695

RAJA YOGA

RAJA YOGA

TEXT, WORD-TO-WORD MEANING, TRANSLATION AND COMMENTARY
OF YOGA SUTRAS OF PATANJALI MAHARSHI BY

Swami Sivananda

Published By

THE DIVINE LIFE SOCIETY
P.O. SHIVANANDANAGAR—249 192
Distt. Tehri-Garhwal, U.P., Himalayas, India

Price]   1999   [Rs. 65/-

First Edition: 1937
Second Edition: 1950
Third Edition: 1999
(3,000 Copies)

**Printed in recognition of the meritorious services
rendered to the Divine Life Society by
the Devotees of Trinidad
(1,000 Copies)**

ISBN 81-7052- 152-1

Published by Swami Krishnananda for The Divine Life Society,
Shivanandanagar, and printed by him at the Yoga-Vedanta
Forest Academy Press, P.O. Shivanandanagar, Distt. Tehri-
Garhwal, U.P., Himalayas, India

H.H. SWAMI SIVANANDAJI MAHARAJ

ॐ

DEDICATED

to

HIRANYAGARBHA — THE FOUNDER

and

PATANJALI MAHARSHI — THE EXPONENT

of

RAJA YOGA PHILOSOPHY

PUBLISHERS' NOTE

The Yoga Sutras of Patanjali Maharshi are the standard Text on Yoga and these Sutras constitute a philosophy as well as a practical technique of meditation. The purpose of the Yoga way of analysis is an overcoming of the limitations of both subjectivity and objectivity and a union of the deepest within us and the deepest in the Cosmos. Yoga is not one way of living among many. It is the only way—gathering of your personality with one purpose. The removal of the idea of externality of the object is the process of meditation. There are certain misconceptions about Yoga. It is not magic or feat of any kind, mental or physical. It is based on a sound philosophy and deep psychology. It is an education process by which the human mind is trained to become more and more natural and weaned from the unnatural conditions of life.

Very few authentic commentaries on the Yoga Sutras are available today. And, the aspirants in this science-minded world of today take a keener interest in this Branch of Yoga. All the Western Sadhakas take to the practice of Raja Yoga. In Europe and America, hundreds of men and women Sadhakas owe their progress in the practice of Raja Yoga to the practical and efficient guidance of Sri Swami Sivanandaji Maharaj. Sri Swamiji's approach is direct, clear and positive.

There has been a persistent demand for a reprint of Sri Swamiji's Raja Yoga. We are happy now to be able to present the readers with a reprint of this precious volume.

28th July, 1999　　　　　　　　　—THE DIVINE LIFE SOCIETY
Sri Guru Purnima

ॐ

पतञ्जलिव्यासमुखानगुरूननन्यांश्च   भक्तितः ।
नतोस्मि वाङ्मनःकायैरज्ञानध्वान्तभास्करान् ॥

We offer our obeisance by word, mind and
body to Patanjali, Vyasa and to all other Rishis
and Yogic Masters, who are like so many suns
to remove the darkness of Ajnana.

ॐ

INSTRUCTIONS OF SANKARA

नलिनीदलगतसलिलंतरलं
तद्वज्जीवितमतिशयचपलम् ।
विद्धि व्याध्यभिमानग्रस्तं
लोकं शोकहतं च समस्तम् ॥ १

Know that this life is most transient and changing like
water on a lotus leaf and that all people suffer from
disease, egoism and miseries.

प्राणायामं प्रत्याहारं
नित्यानित्यविवेकविचारम् ।
जाप्यसमेतसमाधिविधानं
कुर्ववधानं महदवधानम् ॥ २

Engage yourself in right earnest to the practice of control of breath and abstraction of senses and to the discrimination between the real and the unreal and also to the practice of Samadhi along with recitation of Mantra — bestow great attention to these.

का तेऽष्टादशदेशे चिंता

वातुल तव किं नास्ति नियंता ।

यस्त्वां हस्ते सुदृढनिबद्धं

बोधयति प्रभवादि विरुद्धम् ॥ ३

Why is your mind wandering in various directions with anxieties, O peaceless man? Is there no one to guide you, who, catching hold of your hands steadfastly, can cause true knowledge to dawn in you by explaining creation, destruction, etc.?

गुरुचरणांबुजनिर्भरभक्तः

संसारादचिराद्भव मुक्तः ।

सेंद्रियमानसनियमादेवं

द्रक्ष्यसि निजहृदयस्थं देवम् ॥ ४

Get yourself free from the Samsara (wheel of birth and death) by taking shelter at the Lotus Feet of your Guru; and realise the Self in your heart by controlling the senses and the mind.

ॐ

SADGURU STOTRA

गुरुरादिरनादिश्च गुरुपरमदैवतम् ।
गुरोः परतरंनास्ति तस्मै श्री गुरवे नमः ॥

The Guru is the beginning; yet he is without a beginning; the Guru is the Supreme Lord; there is no other than the Guru; Salutations to that Guru.

शोषनं भवसिंधोश्च प्रापनं सारसंपदः ।
यस्यपादोदकंसम्यक् तस्मै श्री गुरवे नमः ॥

Salutations to that Guru, whose 'Charanamrita' dries up the ocean of Samsara and enables one to acquire the essential wealth of the Atman.

नमस्ते सते ते जगत्कारणाय
नमस्ते चिते सर्वलोकाश्रयाय ।
नमो अद्वैततत्त्वाय मुक्तिप्रदाय
नमो ब्रह्मणे व्यापिने शाश्वताय ॥

Salutations to Brahman who is an embodiment of the Truth, the cause for this world, the embodiment of wisdom, the support for all worlds, one without a second, giver of Moksha, who is all-pervading and who is eternal.

CONTENTS

CHAPTER I

WHAT IS YOGA?

CHAPTER II

YOGA SADHANA

CHAPTER III

YAMA

CHAPTER IV

NIYAMA

CHAPTER V

BHAKTI IN YOGA

CHAPTER VI

ASANA

CHAPTER XI

SAMYAMA

CHAPTER XII

DHYANA

ॐ

INTRODUCTION

(1) What Is Raja Yoga

Raja Yoga is the king of all Yogas. It concerns directly with the mind. In this Yoga there is no struggling with Prana or physical body. There are no Hatha Yogic Kriyas. The Yogi sits at ease, watches his mind and silences the bubbling thoughts. He stills the mind and restrains the thought-waves and enters into the thoughtless state or Asamprajnata Samadhi. Hence the name Raja Yoga. Though Raja Yoga is a dualistic philosophy and treats of Prakriti and Purusha, it helps the student in Advaitic Realisation of oneness eventually. Though there is the mention of Purusha, ultimately the Purusha becomes identical with the Highest Self or Brahman of the Upanishads. Raja Yoga pushes the student to the highest rung of the spiritual ladder, Advaitic Realisation of Brahman.

(2) The Author

Patanjali Maharshi is the exponent of Yoga Philosophy. Now Patanjali is regarded as the last of the Avataras. You will find in Yajnavalkya Smriti that Hiranyagarbha was the original teacher of Yoga. Patanjali Maharshi is only a compiler or explainer of the Yogic precepts, doctrines and tenets taught by Hiranyagarbha.

(3) Yoga Sutras

Patanjali Yoga Philosophy is written in Sutras. A 'Sutra' is a terse verse. It is an aphoristic saying. It is pregnant with deep, hidden significance. Rishis of yore have expressed the philosophical ideas and their realisation in the form of Sutras only. It is very difficult to understand the meaning of the Sutras without the help of a commentary, a gloss or a teacher who is well-versed in Yoga. A Yogi with full realisation can explain the Sutras beautifully. Literally, Sutra means a thread. Just as various kinds of flowers with different colours are nicely arranged in a string to make a garland, just as rows of pearls are beautifully arranged in a string to form a necklace, so also Yogic ideas are well arranged in Sutras. They are arranged into Chapters.

(4) The First Chapter

The first Chapter is Samadhipada. It deals with different kinds of Samadhi. It contains 51 Sutras. Obstacles in meditation, five kinds of Vrittis and their control, three kinds of Vairagya, nature of Isvara, various methods to enter into Samadhi and the way to acquire peace of mind by developing virtues are described here.

(5) The Second Chapter

This is Sadhanapada. It contains 55 Sutras. It treats of Kriya Yoga viz., Tapas, study and self-surrender to God, the five Kleshas, the methods to destroy these afflictions which stand in the way of getting Samadhi, Yama and Niyama and their fruits, practice of Asana and its benefits, Pratyahara and its advantage, etc.

(6) The Third Chapter

The third Chapter is Vibhutipada. It contains 56 Sutras. It treats of Dharana, Dhyana and various kinds of Samyama on external objects, mind, internal Chakras and on several objects to acquire various Siddhis.

(7) The Fourth Chapter

The fourth Chapter is Kaivalyapada or Independence.

It contains 34 Sutras. It treats of the Independence of a full-blown Yogi who has perfect discrimination between Prakriti and Purusha, and who has separated himself from the three Gunas. It also deals with mind and its nature. Dharmamegha Samadhi also is described here.

(8) A New Order

The original Yoga Sutras of Patanjali Maharshi are given in the above order into four Chapters. But this book presents a new classification of the subject matter. I have divided the above into fourteen Chapters to render the subject very, very clear and attractive. By so doing many repetitions and confusions are avoided. By the present arrangement, it is very easy to remember the Sutras and the different headings and subject matter connected with each heading. The Raja Yoga philosophy is now rendered attractive and easy for digestion and assimilation. The eight limbs of Raja Yoga viz., Yama, Niyama, Asana, Pranayama, Pratyahara, Dharana, Dhyana and Samadhi are treated separately under 8 Chapters along with many other Chapters on Yoga Sadhana, Mind, Its Mysteries and Control, etc. The word-to-word meaning will be of immense use for the students in understanding the meaning of the Sutra. The Chapter on mind in 6 Sections will help the student much in his practical Sadhana. I have added copious annotations and commentary under each Sutra. This will throw a flood of light wherever the students come across with abstruse, knotty and intricate points on Yoga. This book will supply a long-felt want. It has its own charm, beauty and attractive features. In the Appendix D, the original Sutras in Sanskrit in 4 Chapters are given in order for easy reference of the students. Page number with reference to the Sutras is also given. There will be no difficulty at all in finding out any particular Sutra.

(9) The Yogic Charlatans

A Yogi came to Calcutta and exhibited in the University the feats of drinking pure Nitric acid, swallowing nails and chewing glass pieces. My friend Sri Srinivasa Poddar was present on the occasion. People were struck with wonder. He licked the Nitric acid like honey. But he was a purely commercial man. He made a demonstration of these feats to any one who could pay Rs. 30. Can there be any iota or grain of spirituality or real Yoga where business transactions are made? I leave this for the readers to judge. The poor Yogi died in Rangoon on account of some carelessness in his Kriya. There is nothing really extraordinary in these feats. It is mere Sammohana Vidya, Indrajala or Preta-vidya. There are some herbs to destroy the evil effects of acids and glass pieces. Such feats are not a symptom of spiritual knowledge. Living for four hundred years also is not a sure criterion of advanced spirituality. Through Indrajala one can erect a splendid palace with electric lights and other fittings. One man used to emit light from his anus. He had this Siddhi. He misused this power in evil ways and had a downfall. Possession of Siddhis is not a sign of Self-realisation or spiritual advancement.

(10) Siddhis

I do not deny the true powers of a developed Yogi. Sri Dattatreya created a woman through his Yogic powers. Queen Chudalai created a false husband out of her Yogic power to test her husband Sikhidhvaja. Trailinga Swami, Sri Jnana Dev, Sadasiva Brahman and others had tremendous powers. But there are many Yogic charlatans who deceive the public with some false exhibitions for getting money, fame and name. A real spiritual man will never demonstrate any Siddhi. But he may at times exhibit some power just to convince his students or to bring good

xx

to the public. Chudalai appeared before her husband Sikhidhvaja and stood a few feet above the ground. Sikhidhvaja was quite astonished and took Chudalai as his Guru. Matsyendranath did many miracles to convince Gorakhnath in the truth of Yogic practices. Lord Jesus also exhibited many miracles to convince his disciples.

(11) Samadhi

A Hatha Yogi gets himself buried in a box underneath the ground. He does this by plugging the nostrils through Khechari Mudra. This is no doubt a difficult Kriya. He gets Jada Samadhi. This is a state like deep sleep. The Samskaras and Vasanas are not fried by this Samadhi. He does not return with super-intuitional knowledge. This cannot give Mukti. This is a kind of feat only. This is not a sign of spirituality. People use this Kriya for acquiring money, name and fame. This has become a commercial business. When they come out of the box, they stretch their hands for money. They make transactions before they enter the box. When the Yogi enters into the box, the head must be shaved. When he comes out after his Samadhi, there will not be any growth of hair if it is real Khechari Mudra.

(12) Indrajala

Tie the hands and legs of a man with iron chains and shut him in a room. Before you lock the room he will be standing before you. No doubt this is very astonishing. But it is a mere trick. It is a kind of Jalam. A man throws a rope in the air and ascends in the air. All people are actually witnessing. But when photographed, there will be no picture on the plate. This is a trick and a Jalam. Some people can sit on a plank studded with sharpened nails and can chew snakes likes chocolates. If you pierce a long needle in their arms, no blood will come out. Some can draw water from stone. A real Yogi and a Yogic charlatan can perform all these things. A real Yogi does through his Yogic powers for certain good purpose in view but a charlatan does through some trick or Jalam for the sake of little money, name or fame.

(13) Pseudo Yogis

The public will take a man to be spiritual only if he exhibits some Siddhis. It is a sad, serious mistake. They must be over-credulous. They will be easily duped by these Yogic charlatans. They must use their power of discrimination and reasoning. They must study their nature, ways, habits, conduct, Vritti, Svabhava, antecedence, etc., and test their knowledge of scriptures, before they come to any definite conclusion. Beware of Yogic charlatans!

(14) Importance of Yoga

Practice of Yoga annihilates all the pains of Samsara. Yoga and Jnana are the two wings of the bird of Moksha. Jnana (book knowledge) without Yoga (direct intuitive perception) is useless. Yoga (mere knowledge of Asanas, Mudras, Neti, Dhauti, etc.) without Jnana (Anubhava Jnana) is not perfect. Jnana arises through Yoga (union with Supreme Self). Jnana is the fruit of Yoga. Jnana without Yoga is useless. Yoga without Jnana is dry and barren. Raja Yoga is the Science of sciences. Lord Krishna says: "Kingly science, kingly secret, supreme purifier, this. Intuitional according to righteousness, very, very easy to perform, imperishable."

(15) Unconscious Raja Yogis

Those who invented aeroplanes, steam-engines, motor-cars, railways, wireless, telegraphy, television, gramophone, talkies, etc., are really unconscious Raja

Yogis. They had intense concentration and very sharp intellect. But there is this difference between these materialistic Raja Yogis and Adhyatmic Raja Yogis. Inventors work with a Vyavaharic gross intellect or practical reason of Kant or Asuddha Manas of the Upanishads, or the instinctive mind or Kama Manas of the Theosophists. On the contrary, Raja Yogis work with a subtle, pure intellect, with a Chitta that is purified through the practice of Yama and Niyama. The mind works in the external grooves in the former and in internal grooves in the latter. If the same energy utilised by the inventors is turned inward in the internal grooves in introspection, self-analysis, self-examination and concentration on the Self, they will turn out as marvellous Raja Yogis in a short time.

(16) Siddha Jnanis

The world demands Siddha Jnanis or Yogi Jnanis like Bhagavan Sri Sankaracharya. Kevala Jnani is one who is not able to help the world much but who has obtained Self-realisation for himself. He is good for himself only. He is like a star which glitters at night only. He is not known to the world at large. But a Siddha Jnani or Yogi-Jnani is a glorious person who like the sun shines in the world. He is a Jnani who has Siddhis as well. He is a Jnani and Yogi combined. He can help the world immensely. Sri Sankaracharya, Jesus Christ, Buddha were all Siddha Jnanis.

(17) Conclusion

You too can become a Sankara, Buddha or a Jesus by right kind of Sadhana. You have all the materials within you. You will have to start some sort of spiritual Sadhana now in right earnest. Rise up. Be energetic. May God bless you with spiritual strength, peace, Ananda and Kaivalya (final beatitude). Let me remind you the words of Lord Krishna: "The Yogi is greater than the ascetic; he is thought to be greater than the wise; the Yogi is also greater than the men of action; therefore, become thou a Yogi." I earnestly request you all to become a real Yogi. *"Sarveshu Kaleshu Yogayukto Bhava!"* This is my sincere prayer.

(18) The First Sutra

अथ योगानुशासनम् । I-1

अथ now, योग of Yoga, अनुशासनम् exposition.

Now an exposition of Raja Yoga will be given.

NOTES

This is the first Sutra. Yoga means union or yoke. Yoga is a method by which the individual soul becomes united with the Supreme Soul, the Reality that underlies this universe. Yoga also is defined as an effort to separate the Reality from the apparent. Now I will proceed to explain the system of Raja Yoga philosophy in detail with word by word meaning and explanatory notes on all the Sutras of Patanjali Maharshi, and bring home the salient and vital points in the Yoga system.

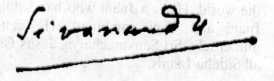

RAJA YOGA

CHAPTER I

WHAT IS YOGA?

1. Yoga Defined

योगश्चित्तवृत्तिनिरोधः । I-2[1]

योगः Yoga, चित्त of the mind-stuff, वृत्ति modifications, निरोधः suppression.

Yoga is the suppression of the modifications of the mind-stuff.

NOTES

The term 'Yoga' comes from the root 'Yuj', which means 'to join.' In its spiritual sense, it is the process by which the identity of the Jivatma and Paramatma is realised by the Yogin. The Jivatma is united with Paramatma by the practice of Yoga. Yoga means union with the Lord. This is the goal of human life. It is the be-all and end-all of human existence. It is the *summum bonum*. Yoga also means 'addition.' When Jivatma is added to Paramatma, the restless Jivatma finds eternal rest and supreme satisfaction. The science that teaches us the way of acquiring this occult knowledge is called Yoga Sastra.

Yoga is the Adhyatmic science that teaches the method of joining the human spirit with God. Yoga is the Divine science which disentangles the Jiva from the phenomenal world of sense-objects and links him with the Absolute, whose inherent attributes are Ananta Ananda, Parama Santi, infinite knowledge, unbroken joy and eternal life.

Yoga in a generic sense refers to Karma Yoga, Bhakti Yoga, Raja Yoga, Jnana Yoga, Hatha Yoga, Mantra Yoga, Laya Yoga or Kundalini Yoga. In a restricted sense it

---

1 Refers to the original order of Sutras.

(3)

means the Ashtanga Yoga or Raja Yoga of Patanjali Maharshi.

The word Yoga is also applicable in a secondary sense to all those factors that go to constitute Yoga that are conducive to the final achievement or fulfilment of Yoga, and as such indirectly lead to final freedom or perfection. A Yogi is one who has reached the final Asamprajnata Samadhi. One who is attempting to get perfection in Yoga is also called a Yogi. How this Yoga is attained, is given in the subsequent pages. Now we shall see the next word 'Chitta Vritti.'

'Chitta' means 'mind-stuff' or subconscious mind. It takes forms or shapes. These forms constitute Vrittis. It gets transformed or modified (Parinama). These transformations or modifications are the thought-waves, whirl-pools or Vrittis. If the Chitta thinks of a mango, the Vritti of a mango is formed in the lake of the Chitta at once, then and there. This will subside and another Vritti will be formed when it thinks of milk. Countless such Vrittis are rising and subsiding in the ocean of the Chitta. These Vrittis are the cause of the restlessness of the mind.

Here, 'Chitta' corresponds to Antahkarana of Vedanta. It is a separate faculty or category in Vedanta. In Vedanta, when the mind does the function of Smriti, Anusandhana and Dharana (memory, enquiry and concentration), it assumes the name Chitta. The functions of Chitta are Smriti or Smarana, Anusandhana and Dharana. When you repeat the Mantra during Japa, it is the Chitta that does the Smarana. It does a lot of work. Much of your subconsciousness consists of submerged experiences, memories thrown into the background but easily recoverable.

Sometimes, you go to sleep at 10 p.m. with the thought: "I must get up at 2 a.m. to catch the train." This message is taken up by the subconscious mind and it is this subconscious mind that wakes you up unfailingly at the exact hour. Subconscious mind is your constant companion and sincere friend. You repeatedly fail at night to get a solution in Arithmetic or Geometry. In the morning when you wake up, you get a clear answer. This comes like a flash from the subconscious mind. Even in sleep it works without any rest. It arranges, classifies, compares, sorts all facts and works out a proper satisfactory solution.

With the help of the subconscious mind you can change your vicious nature by cultivating healthy, virtuous qualities that are opposed to the undesirable ones. If you want to overcome fear, mentally deny that you have fear and concentrate your attention upon the ideal of courage. When courage is developed, fear vanishes away by itself. The positive always overpowers the negative. This is an infallible law of nature. This is Pratipaksha Bhavana of Raja Yogis. You can establish new habits, new ideals, new ideas, new tastes and new character in the subconscious mind by changing the old ones. The Pratipaksha Bhavana method is dealt with in the subsequent Sutras.

The term 'memory' is used in two senses. We say: "Mr. John has got a good memory." Here, it means, that Mr. John's capacity of the mind to store up its past experiences is very good. Sometimes we say: "I have no memory of that incident." Here you cannot bring up to the surface of the conscious mind the incident in its original form that took place some years ago: It is an act of remembering. If the experience is fresh you can have a complete recall of your past experience through memory. You do not get any new knowledge through memory. It is only a reproduction.

Suppose, you have received a nice fan from your amiable friend. When you use the fan, it sometimes reminds you of your friend. You think of him for a short time. This fan serves as Udbhodaka or Smriti-hetu (cause for memory). If your brother is a tall man, the sight of a similar man in another place will bring to your mind the memory of your brother. This is memory due to the similarity of objects (Sadrisyata).

Suppose, you have seen a dwarf at Madras. When you see a very tall man or Patagonian, this will remind you of the dwarf whom you saw at Madras. The sight of a big palace will remind you of a peasant's hut or a Sannyasin's grass-hut on the banks of the Ganga. This memory is due to dissimilarity in objects (Vipareetata).

The following are the four good characteristics of good memory: (1) If you read a passage once and if you can repeat the same nicely, it is a sign to indicate that you have a good memory. This is termed Sugamata. (2) If you can reproduce the same thing without increase or decrease, it is called Araihalya. (3) If you can preserve a fact or passage or anything in your mind for a considerable period, it is called Dharana (retentive memory). (4) If you can repeat a passage at once without any difficulty, when it is needed, it is called Upaharaha.

When you walk along the road on a stormy day, and happen to see a fallen tree, you conclude that the tree has fallen owing to the storm. In this case, the memory is due to the relation between cause and effect (Karya-karana-smbandha).

When you show symptoms of losing your memory, as you grow old, the first symptom is that you find it difficult to remember the names of persons. The reason is not far to seek. All the names are arbitrary. They are like lables. There is no association along with the names. The mind generally remembers through association, as the impressions become deep thereby. You can remember well in old age, some passages that you have studied in schools and colleges. But, you find it difficult to remember in the evening a new passage you have read in the morning. The reason is that the mind has lost its Dharana Sakti (power of grasping ideas). The brain cells have been degenerated. Those who overwork mentally, who do not observe the rules of Brahmacharya and who are afflicted with much cares, worries and anxieties lose their power of memory soon.

The mental processes are not limited to the field of consciousness alone. The field of subconscious mentation is of a much greater extent than that of conscious mentation. Messages when ready, come out like a flash from the subconscious mind to the surface of the conscious mind through the trap door in the subconscious mind or Chitta. Only 10 per cent of mental activities comes into the field of consciousness. At least ninety percent of our mental life is subconscious. We sit and try to solve a problem and fail. We walk around, try again and again fail. When the subconscious processes are at work, suddenly an idea dawns, that leads to the solution of the problem.

When you desire to remember a thing, you will have to make a psychic exertion. You will have to go up and down into the depths of the different levels of subconsciousness and then pick up the right thing from a curious mixture of multifarious, irrelevant matter. Just as the Railway sorter in the Railway Mail Service takes up the right letter by moving his hands up and down along the different pigeon holes, so also the sorter — subconscious mind, goes up and down along the pigeon holes in the subconscious mind and brings the right thing to the level of normal consciousness. The subconscious mind can pick up the right thing from a heap of various matters.

It is obvious, of course, that the powers of remembering from one birth to another, might be a great importance historically, as regards both character and action, but it is difficult to acquire, and when acquired, is not essential for Self-realisation. A close study and thorough knowledge of the functions of Chitta is of immense help to the students of Raja Yoga. The chapter on "Mind" will throw much light on this subject.

'Vritti' means literally a 'whirlpool'. It is a thought-wave in the lake of Chitta. Modification of the mind is known as 'Parinama.' When milk is changed into curd, it is a Parinama. Even so, the mind gets modified into a Vritti by assuming actually the form of the object it perceives. Knowledge of objects or perception is a kind of transformation (Parinama) of the mind.

Why do Vrittis arise from the Chitta? Because of the Samskaras or Vasanas. If you annihilate all Vasanas or desires, all Vrittis will subside by themselves. If all the Vrittis subside, the mind becomes calm, serene and silent. Then alone you will enjoy peace and bliss. Therefore all happiness lies within. You will have to get it through control of mind and not through money, women, children, name and fame, or rank and power.

When the Vritti subsides, it leaves a definite impression in the sub-conscious mind. It is known as Samskara or latent impression. The sum total of all Samskaras is known as Karmasaya (receptacle of works) or Sanchita Karma (accumulated works). When the soul leaves the physical body it carries with it the astral body of seventeen Tattvas and the Karmasaya as well to the mental plane. This Karmasaya is burnt in toto by the highest knowledge obtained through Nirvikalpa Samadhi.

A Samskara of an experience is formed or developed in the Chitta at the very moment that the mind is experiencing something. There is no gap between the present experience and the formation of a Samskara in the subconscious mind.

All actions, enjoyments and experiences leave the impressions in the subconscious mind in the form of subtle impressions or residual potencies. The Samskaras are the roots for causing again Jati (species), life and experiences of pleasure and pain. Revival of Samskaras induce memory. The Yogi dives deep inside and comes in direct contact with these Samskaras. He directly perceives them.

The thinking principle (Chitta) is a comprehensive

expression equivalent to the Sanskrit term "Antahkarana." Antahkarana means inner instrument. Antahkarana is a broad term used in Vedanta. It includes Manas, Buddhi, Chitta and Ahamkara.

Manas is Sankalpa-vikalpatmaka (willing and doubting). It thinks: "whether to go to a place or not; whether to do this or not; whether this is good or bad." The mind is of doubting nature. It is the Buddhi or the light that determines one way or other. Buddhi is Nischayatmaka. It is the determining faculty. The mind, intellect and egoism are various process in the mind-stuff. Ahamkara is the self-asserting principle. It does the function of Abhimana. It creates "Mamata" or "mineness." This is the root cause for all human sufferings. All Vrittis hang on this one Vritti, "Aham Vritti." It is the root cause for human ignorance.

Now comes the word Nirodha. It means restraint or suppression. By suppressing the modifications of the mind-stuff or restraining of the thought-waves, a man obtains Yoga. Patanjali Maharshi has given the whole Raja Yoga in this one Sutra. Different methods of Sadhana are intended to achieve the highest stage of Yoga, Asamprajnata Samadhi by the suppression of the thought-wave. The Yogi tries to stop all the Vrittis. He tries to make the mind blank. He tries to stop thinking. He practises thoughtlessness. He stops the mind from assuming various forms. This is called "Chitta Vritti Nirodha." This is the path of Raja Yoga. Suppression of thought waves is easily said. But it is very difficult indeed to practice. How this is being successfully done is explained in the rest of the pages.

2. Object of Yoga

तदा द्रष्टुः स्वरूपेऽवस्थानम् । I-3

तदा then, द्रष्टुः the seer, स्वरूपे in his own nature, अवस्थानम् abiding, resting.

Then, the seer rests in his own nature.

NOTES

Although the mind is one, it passes into many conditions or states, as it is made up of three qualities, Gunas, viz., Sattva, Rajas and Tamas. All these qualities enter into a variety of combinations. So, the modifications or Vrittis of the mind are also various. Peace of mind (Santa Vritti) is a Sattvic Vritti. Lust is a Rajasic Vritti. Laziness is a Tamasic Vritti. Anger is a Ghora Vritti.

Internal fight is ever going on between Gunas, Sattva, Rajas and Tamas; between good Vrittis and evil Vrittis. This is the internal warfare between Suras and Asuras.

When the lake is in a boisterous state on account of the turbulent waves, you can hardly see the bottom of the lake. When the waves subside, you can clearly see the bottom of the lake. Even so when the mind is in an agitated condition on account of various Vrittis, you can hardly rest in your own nature. You cannot see or realise your own Self. But when the Vrittis subside, you can rest in your own state. You do not identify yourself with the Vrittis now. "Then" means "when all the Vrittis subside" or done through Chitta Vritti Nirodha.

By suppressing the transformations of the mind, the Sadhaka acquires great Siddhis. He becomes an adept or a great Siddha. Yoga is a complete suppression of the tendency of the mind to transform itself into objects, thoughts, etc. It demands continuous and steady practice. Then comes unlimited strength, peace, bliss and knowledge. This leads to Asamprajnata Samadhi and Kaivalya, the highest stage of Raja Yoga.

CHAPTER II

YOGA SADHANA

1. Hints on Sadhana

Sadhana means any spiritual practice that helps the Sadhaka to realise God. Abhyasa and Sadhana are synonymous terms. Sadhana is a means to attain the goal of human life. Without Sadhana no one can achieve the purpose of life. Sadhana differs in different individuals according to the capacity, temperament and taste. Everyone must take to some kind of Sadhana to attain the state of final beatitude. Sadhya is that which is attained through Sadhana. It is God or Atman or Purusha. If you want to evolve quickly you must have the right kind of Sadhana. If you are a student of the path of self-reliance, you can yourself select the Sadhana for your daily practice. If you are a student of the path of self-surrender, you should get the right kind of Sadhana from a Guru and practise the same with intense faith.

2. Bhakti Yoga Sadhana

Those who follow the path of devotion should do Japa, Read the holy scriptures such as the Bhagavata or the Ramayana. By the practice of Navavidha Bhakti, the Bhakta should develop Bhakti to a very high degree. Sravana, Smarana, Kirtana, Vandana, Archana, Padasevana, Sakhya, Dasya and Atma Nivedana are the nine methods to develop Bhakti. Bhaktas should observe Vrata, Anushthana and do prayers and Manasic Puja. They should serve others, realising that the Lord resides in the hearts of all. This is the Sadhana for those who tread the path of Bhakti Yoga.

3. Hatha Yoga Sadhana

The students of Hatha Yoga should try to awaken the Kundalini Sakti that lies dormant in the Muladhara Chakra by Mudras, Bandhas, Asanas and Pranayama. They should try to unite the Prana and Apana and send the united Prana-apana through the Sushumna Nadi. Heat is increased by retention of breath and Vayu ascends up along with Kundalini to the Sahasrara Chakra through the different Chakras. When Kundalini is united with Lord Siva at the Sahasrara Chakra, the Yogi attains supreme peace, bliss and immortality.

4. Karma Yoga Sadhana

Those who follow the path of Karma Yoga should do disinterested selfless service to the suffering humanity and society in various ways. They should surrender the fruits of action to the Lord as Isvararpana. They should give up agency by realising that they are the instruments in the hands of God. They should get rid of their selfishness and control their Indriyas. They should completely consecrate their lives in the service of humanity. They should consider that the whole world is a manifestation of the Lord. If they serve people with such a Bhava, their hearts get purified in the long run. Eventually they get knowledge of the Self through Chitta Suddhi. This is the Sadhana for the Karma Yogins. This is very important for all beginners in the spiritual path. This is the first step in the spiritual path. This is not the goal itself. Many erroneously think so and neglect the higher courses of Sadhana. They should advance still further and through Dharana, Dhyana and Samadhi, reach the highest goal.

5. Raja Yoga Sadhana

A Raja Yogi slowly ascends the Yogic ladder through the eight steps. He gets ethical training in the beginning to purify himself by the practice of Yama and he practises Niyama. Then he steadies his posture. Then he practises

Pranayama to steady his mind and purify the Nadis. Then by the practice of Pratyahara, Dharana and Dhyana he gets Samadhi. Through Samyama he gets different Siddhis. He restrains all the mental modifications that arise from the mind. Detailed instructions on this subject are given in the subsequent pages.

6. Jnana Yoga Sadhana

Those who take up the path of Vedanta or Jnana Yoga should acquire first the four means of salvation (Sadhana Chatushtaya): Viveka, Vairagya, Shat Sampat and Mumukshutva. Viveka is discrimination between the real and the unreal. Vairagya is indifference to sensual enjoyments. Shat Sampat or sixfold virtue consists of: Sama (serenity of mind), Dama (control of the Indriyas), Uparati (satiety), Titiksha (power of endurance), Sraddha (intense faith) and Samadhana (mental balance). Mumukshutva is intense desire for liberation. Then they approach a Brahmanishtha Guru who has realised the Supreme Self and hear the Srutis from him. Then they reflect and meditate on the Self and eventually attain Atma Sakshatkara. Then the Jnani exclaims with joy: "The Atman alone is, one without a second. Atman alone is the one Reality. I am Brahman. Aham Brahma Asmi. Sivoham. Sarvam Khalvidam Brahma." The liberated sage (Jivanmukta) sees the Self in all beings and all beings in the Self.

7. Hatha Yoga and Raja Yoga

Hatha Yoga concerns with the physical body and control of breath. Raja Yoga deals with the mind. Raja Yoga and Hatha Yoga are inter-dependent. Raja Yoga and Hatha Yoga are the necessary counterparts of each other. No one can become a perfect Yogi without a knowledge of the practice of both the Yogas. Raja Yoga begins where properly practised Hatha Yoga ends. A Hatha Yogi starts his Sadhana with his body and Prana; a Raja Yogi starts his

Sadhana with mind; and a Jnana Yogi starts his Sadhana
with Buddhi and will. A Hatha Yogi gets different kinds of
Siddhis when the Kundalini reaches the different Chakras.
A Raja Yogi gets Siddhis by his Yogic Samyama by
combined practice of Dharana, Dhyana and Samadhi at
one and the same time.

8. Different Paths

The spiritual path is thorny, precipitous and keen like
the edge of a razor, but nevertheless has been trodden by
men of strong determination, undaunted spirit and
indomitable energy. When once you make up your mind to
tread the path, everything becomes smooth and easy.
There is descent of grace from the Lord. The whole
spiritual world will back you up. The path will directly take
you to the realms of Infinite Bliss.

Just as one coat will not suit Mr. John, Mr. Tom,
Mr. Banerjee or Mr. Iyer, so also one path will not suit all
people. There are four paths to suit four kinds of
temperament. They all lead to the same goal, the
attainment of ultimate Reality. Roads are different but the
destination is the same. The four paths that are inculcated
for the achievement of this ultimate Truth from the
different standpoints of the man of action or the busy
working man, the emotional or devotional man, the mystic
man, or the philosopher or the man of reason and will, are
respectively termed Karma Yoga, Bhakti Yoga, Raja Yoga
and Jnana Yoga.

The four paths Karma, Bhakti, Raja and Jnana Yoga
are not antagonistic to one another, but on the other hand
are complementary. Religion must educate and develop
the whole man—his heart, intellect (head) and hand. Then
only perfection will come in. One-sided development is not
commendable. Karma Yoga purifies and develops the
hand. Bhakti Yoga destroys Vikshepa and develops the
heart. Raja Yoga steadies the mind and makes it

one-pointed. Jnana Yoga removes the veil of ignorance and develops will and reason. Therefore, one should practise the four Yogas. He can have Jnana Yoga as the central basis and can practise the other Yogas as auxiliaries to bring in rapid progress in the spiritual path.

9. Period of Sadhana

स तु दीर्घकालनैरन्तर्यसत्कारासेवितो दृढभूमिः । I-14

स this (practice), तु and, दीर्घकाल for a long period, नैरन्तर्य without any break, सत्कार with perfect devotion, असेवित: when practised well, दृढभूमि: firm ground, fixed, steady.

Practice becomes firmly grounded when practised for a long time, without any break and with perfect devotion.

NOTES

Constant, steady application is indispensably requisite for perfect control of mind and attainment of Asamprajnata Samadhi which alone can fry all the seeds (Samskaras). Therefore, constant and intense practice is needed for a long period of time. Then only the wandering mind will come under your perfect control. Then only wherever it is directed, it will be ever at rest. Without practise nothing can be achieved. The practice should be accompanied by perfect faith and devotion. If there is no faith and regularity, success in the practice is impossible. The practice should be done till one gets perfect control of mind.

10. What Is Vairagya

दृष्टानुश्रविकविषयवितृष्णस्य वशीकारसंज्ञा वैराग्यम् । I-15

दृष्ट seen, अनुश्रविक heard, scriptural, विषय enjoyments, वितृष्णस्य of him who is free from hankering for, वशीकार control, संज्ञा consciousness, वैराग्यम् non-attachment.

That particular state of mind, which manifests in one who does not hanker for objects seen or heard and in which one is

conscious of having controlled or mastered those objects, is non-attachment.

NOTES

It is only when the mind is absolutely free from attachment of all sorts that true knowledge begins to dawn and Samadhi supervenes. Drishta: perceptible objects are objects of the world. Secret powers, attainment of heaven, states of Videha and Prakritilaya, etc., are scriptural. One should be perfectly free from all sorts of temptations. Samadhi comes by itself when the Yogic student is established in perfect Vairagya. Para Vairagya is the means of Asamprajnata Samadhi. There four stages in Vairagya: (1) *Yatamanam:* This is attempt not to allow the mind run to sensual objects. (2) *Vyatirekam:* Some objects attract you and you are endeavouring to cut off the attachment and attraction. Slowly Vairagya develops for these objects. Then Vairagya matures. When some objects tempt and attract you, you should ruthlessly avoid them. You will have to develop Vairagya for these tempting objects and it must mature also. In this stage you are conscious of your degree of Vairagya towards different objects. (3) *Ekendriyam:* The Indriyas stand still or subdued, but the mind has either Raga or Dvesha for objects. Mind is the only Indriya that functions now independently. (4) *Vasikaram:* In this highest state of Vairagya, the objects no longer tempt you. They cause no attraction. Indriyas are perfectly quiet. Mind also is free from likes and dislikes. Then you get supremacy or independence. You are conscious of your supremacy. Without Vairagya no spiritual progress is possible.

One Anna (1/16th of a Rupee) of pleasure is mixed with fifteen Annas of pain. Pleasure that is mixed with pain, fear and worry is no pleasure at all. If you begin to analyse carefully this one Anna of pleasure, it will dwindle into airy nothing. You will find that it is a mere play of the mind. Wake up. Open your eyes. Develop Viveka. You cannot get the real happiness from finite objects that are conditioned by time, space and causation. Nitya, Nirupadhika, Niratisaya Ananda, eternal, infinite bliss that is independent of objects can only be had in the immortal Spirit or Atman, the Indweller of your heart. Therefore, shun the external things ruthlessly; you can develop Vairagya. Vairagya is the foundation-stone for the spiritual path.

Why do men run after sensual pleasures? What is their idea of happiness? Do Samskaras force them to repeat the same sensual acts? Is man a creature of environment or circumstances? Can he not obliterate the Samskaras by suitable means?

On account of ignorance man runs higher and thither to seek happiness in objects. A little ginger bread and a sweetmeat, a son and a young wife, some position and power and some money in the bank to boot, will fill the heart with joy and will calm his nerves. That is all he wants. Bliss of Atman, supersensuous Ananda and peace, spiritual ecstasy are unknown to him. He dislikes it also. He hates people who talk on higher sublime matters. Man can obliterate his Samskaras by Purushartha (right exertion). He is not a creature of circumstances. He is the master of his destiny.

Amidst the din and boisterous bustle of worldly activities, there come moments of tranquillity and peace, when the mind, for the time being, however short it may be, soars above the filthy worldly things and reflects on the higher problems of life, viz., "Whence? Where? Whither? Why of the universe? Who am I?" The sincere enquirer becomes serious and extends his reflections. He begins to search and understand the Truth. Discrimination dawns on him. He seeks Vairagya, concentration, meditation and purification of body and mind and eventually attains the highest knowledge of the Self. But the man whose mind is saturated with worldly Vasanas is quite heedless and is

irresistibly carried away by the two currents of Raga and
Dvesha and tossed about helplessly in the tumultuous
Samsaric stream of worldly concerns.

How uncertain is sensual life in this world! If you
constantly think of the transitory nature of sensual
pleasure and its concomitant evils of miseries, worries,
troubles, anxieties and premature death, then you can
slowly develop Vairagya. The Vairagya that momentarily
comes out on the loss of wife, children or property, will not
help you much. Vairagya born of discrimination will bring
in spiritual progress.

In the presence of sensual pleasures, spiritual bliss
cannot exist just as darkness cannot exist in the presence of
light. Therefore, show extreme contempt towards all
worldly objects. Destroy desire. Turn the mind away from
the sensual objects. You can develop Vairagya.

11. Para Vairagya

तत्परं पुरुषख्यातेर्गुणवैतृष्ण्यम् । I-16

तत् that, परम् supreme, पुरुषः the Purusha, ख्यातेः due to
the knowledge, गुणः the qualities, वैतृष्ण्यम् non-attachment,
indifference.

**Para Vairagya or supreme non-attachment is that state
wherein even the attachment to the qualities (Sattva, Rajas
and Tamas) drops owing to the knowledge of Purusha.**

NOTES

The Vairagya described in the previous Sutra is
Apara Vairagya (lower one). Now comes supreme
Vairagya. In the former state, there is preponderance of
Sattva. Sattva is mixed with Rajas. But there is absence
of Tamas. The Yogi gets Siddhis and becomes a Videha
or Prakritilaya. The Yogi with Para Vairagya rejects the
Siddhis also and gets Sakshatkara or Darsana of
Purusha. In ordinary Vairágya there is a trace of Vasanas

and Samskaras. But in Para Vairagya, Vasanas and Samskaras are fried in toto. In Para Vairagya there will be no desire at all. Perfect desireless state is Para Vairagya. In the Gita (II-59), you will find: "Objects fall away from the abstinent man, leaving the longing behind. But his longing also ceases, who sees the Supreme." This is the state of Para Vairagya.

12. Auxiliaries to Yoga Sadhana

Though particular stress is not laid in Raja Yoga on certain points, there are some that are very useful for Yoga Sadhana which I will tell you in brief. They are useful to all aspirants.

Food plays a prominent role in Yoga Sadhana. An aspirant should be very careful in the selection of articles of Sattvic nature especially in the beginning period of his Sadhana. Purity of food leads to purity of mind. Sattvic food helps meditation. Milk, ghee, wheat, cream, butter, fruits, etc., are Sattvic articles. Heavy food leads to Tamasic state and induces sleep. Mitahara plays a vital part in keeping up perfect health. A man of Mitahara can tide over a host of ailments. A glutton is quite unfit for Yoga Sadhana.

Places of cool climate are required for Yoga practices. You must select a place where you can stay all through the year, in winter, summer and rainy seasons. You must be in a place where there will be no disturbances. Do not have frequent wanderings from place to place in the beginning of your Sadhana. Select a secluded place. You will have quick progress.

Para Vairagya or the supreme non-attachment is that state, wherein even the attachment to the qualities (Sattva, Rajas and Tamas) drops owing to the knowledge of Purusha.

13. Obstacles in Yoga

व्याधिस्त्यानसंशयप्रमादालस्याविरतिभ्रान्तिदर्शनालब्ध-
भूमिकत्वानवस्थितत्वानि चित्तविक्षेपास्तेऽन्तरायाः । I-30

व्याधि disease, स्त्यान dullness, संशय doubt, प्रमाद carelessness, आलस्य laziness, indolence, अविरति worldlimindedness
or sensuality, भ्रान्ति दर्शन mistaken notion of illusion, अलब्ध
भूमिकत्व missing the point, अनवस्थितत्व instability, चित्तविक्षेपाः
causing distractions of the mind, ते these (are the), अन्तरायाः
obstacles.

**Disease, dullness, doubt, carelessness, laziness, indolence,
worldlimindedness or sensuality, mistaken notion of illusion,
missing the point, instability, causing distractions of the
mind, these are the obstacles.**

NOTES

Diseases arise through the disturbance in the
equilibrium in the three humours, viz., wind, bile and
phlegm. If there is more phlegm, the body becomes heavy.
You cannot sit for a long time in the Asana. If there is
more Tamas in the mind, you become lazy. Diseases may
be due to irregularity in taking food, unwholesome food
that cannot agree with the system, late vigil overnight, loss
of seminal energy, checking the urine and faeces. Diseases
can be removed by the practice of Asana, Pranayama and
physical exercises, meditation, dietetic adjustment, fasting,
purgatives, enema, bath, sun-treatment, sufficient rest, etc.
First diagnose the case and find out the cause for the
disease and then try for a remedy or consult some doctors.

In Styana (dullness), the person is unfit to do any
practice on account of inexperience in the line and lack of
Samskaras in the previous births. It is indisposition of the
mind to work. Dullness, laziness, etc., can be eradicated by
Pranayama, Asana and active habits. Doubt is whether it is
this or that. Such indecisive notion is doubt. The Yogi is
not able to proceed further in the path of Yoga. He will

doubt whether all that is said in the Yoga Sastras is true or not. This can be dispelled by right knowledge, Viveka, Vichara, study of scriptures and by Satsanga with Mahatmas.

Avirati is that tendency of the mind which unceasingly longs keenly for one or the other kind of sensual enjoyment on account of attachment. This is destroyed by Vairagya, looking into the faults of worldly objects and worldly life, such as, impermanence, diseases, death, old age, miseries, etc., and constant Satsanga with dispassionate Mahatmas and study of books on Vairagya.

Bhranti-darshana is mistaking an undesirable state as the most desirable one due to illusion. Missing the point is going astray from the right path, Samadhi, from falling into the clutches of Siddhis. Mistaken notion is removed by Satsanga with Yogins. Missing the point and instability are removed by developing more Vairagya and doing constant and intense Sadhana in seclusion. Anavasthitatva or instability is that fickleness of the mind which does not allow the Yogi to remain in the state of Samadhi, even though he has reached it with great difficulty. Maya is powerful. There is many a slip between the cup and the lip. These obstacles do not come to those who do Japa of OM as stated in Sutra 24 of Chapter II.

When slight difficulties appear, do not stop the practice. Find out suitable means to eradicate the obstacles. Plod on till you get the highest Asamprajnata Samadhi. Success is bound to come if you are sincere and steady in Sadhana.

14. Causes of Distractions

दुःखदौर्मनस्याऽङ्गमेजयत्वश्वासप्रश्वासा विक्षेपसहभुवः ॥ I-31

दुःख pain, दौर्मनस्य despair, अङ्गमेजयत्व tremor of the body, श्वास inhalation, प्रश्वासाः exhalation, विक्षेप oscillation or tossing of mind, सहभुवः companions.

Pain, despair, tremor of the body, inhalation and exhalation are the companions of the causes of distraction (oscillation of mind).

NOTES

The above signs follow in the train of the obstacles enumerated in the Sutra 30 of Chapter I. Pain is that which gives uneasiness for the mind. Despair is the unsteadiness of the mind caused by non-fulfilment of some desire. When the mind is distracted, the inhalation and exhalation are not in a normal condition. There is evidently abnormal state of breathing. In the Gita (II-60) you will find: "The turbulent senses do violently snatch away the mind of even a wise man, striving for perfection." This is distraction. You should be very careful. Have regular, steady and systematic practice of concentration. Do not be unnecessarily alarmed by the above causes of distractions. They will soon pass off by repetition of OM, self-surrender to God and repeated practice in concentration and meditation. Adjust your diet also. Take light, Sattvic, nourishing, substantial food. You will be all right soon. Have perfect trust in God and be steady in your Sadhana. These obstacles come only at other times of concentration. When the seer identifies with his own native state, there cannot arise such obstacles. Refer to Sutra 4 of Chapter I.

15. Remedy for Distractions

तत्प्रतिषेधार्थमेकतत्त्वाभ्यासः । I-32

तत् their, प्रतिषेध prevention, अर्थम् for, एक one, तत्त्व subject, अभ्यासः intense practice.

To prevent these (one should have), intense practice on one subject.

NOTES

Intense concentration on one thing will obviate the above accompaniments of distraction. Increase your Vairagya also. Select any object or form that you like best and fix the mind there for some time. This is Dharana. Steady practice will remove all the obstacles or the stumbling blocks on the way. Refer to the Chapter on Dharana for detailed information. Perfect control of mind and Indriyas is required to completely destroy the distractions. Practice of Trataka or steady gazing at a particular point, is an effective exercise to remove Vikshepa.

CHAPTER III

YAMA

1. Eight Accessories of Yoga

यमनियमासनप्राणायामप्रत्याहारधारणाध्यान-
समाधयोऽष्टावङ्गानि । II-29

यम restraint, नियम religious observances, आसन posture,
प्राणायाम control of breath, प्रत्याहार abstraction of Indriyas,
धारणा concentration, ध्यान meditation, समाधि superconscious
state or trance, अष्टौ eight, अङ्गानि accessories or limbs.

**Restraint, religious observances, posture, control of
breath, abstraction of Indriyas, concentration, meditation,
superconscious state or trance, are the eight accessories of
Yoga.**

NOTES

The eight accessories of Yoga described above are like
the eight steps in the path of Raja Yoga. They all should be
practised in the order given. You will not be benefitted if
you take to the practice of Asanas, Pranayama without
practising Yama, Niyama. Yama and Niyama are the very
foundation of Yoga. The practice of Yama gives
tremendous ethical power. If you want to take up M.Sc.
course, you will have to start from the infant standard, pass
through the different stages of first standard, second
standard and so on and then enter the college course. Even
so, you will have to go stage by stage, step by step, in the
Yogic courses also.

2. Benefits of the Accessories

योगाङ्गानुष्ठानादशुद्धिक्षये ज्ञानदीप्तिराविवेकख्यातेः । II-28

योग of Yoga, अङ्ग (eight) accessories or limbs, अनुष्ठानाद्

the practice, अशुद्धि impurity, क्षये on the destruction, ज्ञानदीप्तिः the light of wisdom, आ leading to, विवेकख्यातेः discriminative knowledge.

On the destruction of the impurities through the practice of the (eight) accessories of Yoga, arises the light of wisdom, leading to the discriminative knowledge.

NOTES

Yama is the practice of Ahimsa, Satyam, Asteya, Brahmacharya and Aparigraha. Niyama is the observance of the five canons, viz., Saucha, Santosha, Tapas, Svadhyaya and Isvarapranidhana. By practising Yama and Niyama, the Yogic student purifies his mind. By practising Asana, he gets steadiness and firmness of body. By practising Pranayama, he removes the tossing of mind and destroys Rajas and Tamas. By practising Pratyahara, he gets mental strength, peace of mind and inner life. By the practice of Dharana, he gets Ekagrata (one-pointed) state of mind. By practising Dhyana, he fills the mind with divine thoughts. By practising Samadhi, he destroys the seeds of births and deaths, and gets immortality and Kaivalya, the final beatitude, the highest end of human life.

By the practice of the eight Angas of Yoga, dirt of the mind[2] (five Klesas) is removed and discrimination of Prakriti-Purusha comes by itself. Then the Yogi attains Kaivalya.

3. What Is Yama

अहिंसासत्यास्तेयब्रह्मचर्यापरिग्रहा यमाः । II-30

अहिंसा abstinence from injury and killing, सत्य truthfulness, आस्तेय abstinence from theft or falsehood, ब्रह्मचर्य continence, अपरिग्रह abstinence from avariciousness, यमाः are the restraints.

(Among these accessories) abstinence from injury and

2 Explained in the chapter on 'MIND'.

killing, truthfulness, abstinence from theft or falsehood, continence, abstinence from avariciousness or greed, are the restraints.

NOTES

Yama is the very foundation of Yoga, without which the superstructure of Yoga cannot be built. Practice of Yama is really the practice of Sadachara (right conduct). The noble eightfold path of Buddhists deals with the practice of Yama only. In every religion you will find this to be the foremost. Manu says: "*Ahimsa satyasteyam sauchamindriya nigraha* — harmlessness, truth speaking, refraining from theft, control of senses; this is the essence of Dharma." Great emphasis is given in every chapter of the Gita on the practice of Yama.

Patanjali Maharshi mentions the above five chief items for practice in Yama. According to Sandilya Rishi, the practice of Saucha, Daya, Arjava, Dhriti and Mitahara is included in Yama. Saucha is external and internal purity. Washing the hands, taking baths, etc., are for external purity. Filling the mind with pure divine thoughts is internal purity. Daya is mercy or compassion, in all places, for all creatures. Arjava is the keeping up of balance of mind while doing actions. Dhriti is fortitude or mental power of endurance. Mitahara is moderation in eating.

4. Universal Vows

जातिदेशकालसमयानवच्छिन्नाः सार्वभौमा महाव्रतम् । II-31

जाति class, देश place, काल time, समय circumstances, अवच्छिन्ना not limited by, सार्वभौमा universal, महाव्रतम् the Great Vows.

(These restraints) are the Great Vows, universal, not limited by class, place, time and circumstances.

NOTES

The restraints are Ahimsa, Satya, Asteya, Brahmacharya and Aparigraha. This Sutra refers to all the

above restraints. Some may have certain conditions and
exemptions in observing certain restraints. One may have a
principle not to kill anything on new moon day. When such
conditions and exemptions are laid down, then the practice
of restraints are not considered to be perfect. They should
not be limited by class, place, time or circumstances. The
restraints should be practised at all times, in all places, by
one and all, in all circumstances. They should be practised
in thought, word and deed.

5. Ahimsa

अहिंसाप्रतिष्ठायां तत्सन्निधौ वैरत्यागः । II-35

अहिंसा abstinence from injuring and killing, प्रतिष्ठायां
being established, तत्सन्निधौ in his (the practitioner's)
presence, वैरत्यागः hostilities are given up.

**Abstinence from injuring and killing, being established, all
hostilities are given up in the presence of the practitioner.**

NOTES

Ahimsa is not causing of pain to any creature in any
way, at any time, in thought, word and deed. The other
restraints that follow have their origin in this. These are
meant to make this restraint perfect. You will not be
benefitted much by taking to the practice of the other four
restraints without the practice of Ahimsa. Giving up of
animal food also comes under Ahimsa, because it is not
obtainable without Himsa of some kind.

If you hurt another man or cause another to commit
injury to others or even approve of another doing so, it is
equally sinful. Action and reaction are equal and opposite.
If you injure another, it is bound to react on you whether in
this moment or at a future date. You will have to suffer
anyhow in return. If you remember this law, you will not
commit any injury.

According to Tilak's school of thought, if by the murder
of a dacoit thousands of lives could be saved, it is not

considered as Himsa. Ahimsa and Himsa are relative terms. Some say that one can defend himself with instruments and use a little violence when he is in danger and this also is not considered to be Himsa. A Sannyasi should not defend himself and use violence even when his life is in jeopardy. English people generally shoot their horses and dogs when they are in acute agony, and when there is no way of relieving their sufferings. They wish that the soul should be immediately freed from the physical body. Motive is the chief factor. It underlies everything. The term 'hostilities are given up' means, that all beings, men, animals, birds and poisonous creatures would approach the practitioner without fear and would do no harm to him. Their hostile nature disappears in them in his presence. The rat and the cat, the snake and the mongoose and others being natural enemies to each other, give up their hostile feelings in the presence of the Yogi who is established in Ahimsa. Lions and tigers can never do any harm to such a Yogi. The wolf and the lamb, the frog and the cobra will play in his presence. Such a Yogi can give definite orders to lions and tigers. They will obey. This is called as Bhuta Siddhi, obtainable by the practice of Ahimsa. The practice of Ahimsa will culminate eventually in realisation of unity and oneness of life, Advaitic consciousness. It will enable one to obtain cosmic love.

6. Satya

सत्यप्रतिष्ठायां क्रियाफलाऽश्रयत्वम् । II-36

सत्य truthfulness, प्रतिष्ठायां being established, क्रिया action, फल fruition, आश्रयत्वं bestowal.

Speaking truth, when established, leads (the Yogi) to the bestowal of fruits for actions.

NOTES

Speaking truth is the most important qualification of a Yogi. In Hitopadesa you will find: "If truth and one thousand Asvamedha Yajnas are weighed in a balance, truth alone will outweigh." In Mahabharata also we find: "The four Vedas on the one side, well studied together with their Angas and Upangas are far outweighed by truth alone on the other." Such is the importance of truth.

God is truth. He can be realised by speaking truth and observing truth in thought, word and deed. Truthfulness, equality, self-control, absence of envious emulation, forgiveness, modesty, endurance, absence of jealousy, charity, thoughtfulness, disinterested philanthropy, self-possession, and unceasing and compassionate harmlessness, are the thirteen forms of truth.

Some persons hold that lie, that is calculated to bring immense good, is regarded as truth. Suppose an unrighteous king has ordered a sage to be hanged without any cause. If the life of this sage can be saved by uttering a falsehood, the falsehood is only truth. These are limited by circumstances. According to Sutra II-31, these restraints should not be limited by class, time, space and circumstances, if one wants to practise them perfectly. By speaking truth always in all circumstances, the Yogi acquires Vak Siddhi. Whatever he thinks or speaks, turns to be true. He can do anything even by mere thought.

7. Asteya

अस्तेयप्रतिष्ठायां सर्वरत्नोपस्थानम् । II-37

अस्तेय non-stealing or abstinence from theft, प्रतिष्ठायां when established, सर्व all kinds of, रत्न wealth, उपस्थानम् approach.

Non-stealing or abstinence from theft, when established, all kinds of wealth approach (the Yogi).

NOTES

The third restraint is in abstaining from theft. The pilfering nature should be completely annihilated. One should be satisfied with what he gets through honest

means. Besides actual illegal appropriation, taking away
the property or things of others, the very thought of any
such gain should not enter the mind. Hoarding money is
really theft. You should not keep anything more than the
actual necessity. Eating more than what is really necessary
is also considered as theft. When a man has powerful
Indriyas and uncontrolled mind, he wants many things for
his own sensual enjoyment. If he could not get the objects
of enjoyment and satisfy his desires, then the pilfering
nature enters his mind. By constant thinking, he does the
actual theft. Therefore the real cause for theft is too many
desires and indisciplined Indriyas. To abstain from theft,
one should slowly curb desires and discipline the Indriyas
and control the mind. In this Sutra it is assured that when
you completely give up the evil habit of theft, then the
desired thing and all kinds of wealth will come to you by
themselves.

8. Brahmacharya

ब्रह्मचर्यप्रतिष्ठायां वीर्यलाभः । II-38

ब्रह्मचर्य celibacy (continence), प्रतिष्ठायां being established,
वीर्य vigour, लाभः gained, obtained.

By the establishment of celibacy, vigour is gained.

NOTES

If semen is preserved by the observance of
Brahmacharya, and transmuted into Ojas Sakti, the
spiritual and intellectual power will increase. This is the
fundamental qualification of an aspirant. Brahmacharya is
the most important virtue for Self-realisation.
Brahmacharya is purity in thought, word and deed. The
very idea of lust should not enter the mind. No Yoga or
spiritual progress is possible without continence. In the
Gita you will find the importance of Brahmacharya in the
IV and VIII chapters. Since I have already given in my
book "Practice of Brahmacharya," various effective

methods for getting established in Brahmacharya, I will
pass on to the next Sutra.

9. Aparigraha

अपरिग्रहस्थैर्ये जन्मकथन्तासंबोधः । II-39

अपरिग्रह abstinence from greed, स्थैर्य being established,
जन्म existence or births, कथंता the how of, संबोधः knowledge.

**When abstinence from greed is established, the knowledge
of the how of existence or births comes.**

NOTES

Aparigraha is freedom from greed or covetousness.
One should not try to keep or try to get in possession
anything beyond the very necessaries of life. Gifts from
others affect the mind of the receiver. As people are
extremely selfish, they make presents with various motives.
These motives affect the receiver. The mind of the receiver
becomes impure by receiving gifts. A student of Yoga
should, therefore, avoid gifts. Attachment, and the anxiety
which accompanies attachment, are obstacles to
knowledge. Freedom from attachment will result in
knowledge of the whole course of our journey. "Who was
I? How was I? What is this? What shall I be? How shall I
be?" In this shape comes to him the knowledge of his own
experience in the past, present and future. He becomes
independent and free. His mind becomes pure. Everything
becomes quite clear to him. He gets a memory of past life
also.

CHAPTER IV

NIYAMA

1. What Is Niyama

शौचसन्तोषतपः स्वाध्यायेश्वरप्रणिधानानि नियमाः । II-32

शौच internal and external purity, सन्तोष contentment, तपः mortification, स्वाध्याय study of scriptures, ईश्वरप्रणिधानानि worship of God or self-surrender, नियमाः observances.

The observances are (the practice of) internal and external purity, contentment, mortification, study of scriptures and worship of God or self-surrender

NOTES

Niyama is the second accessory of Yoga. It is the practice of purity, contentment, mortification, study and worship. Patanjali Maharshi mentions these five observances under Niyama. According to Sandilya Rishi, Tapas, Santosha, Astikya, Dana, Isvara Pujana, Siddhanta Sravana, Hrih, Mati, Japa and Vrata come under Niyama. Through the practice of Krichara and Chandrayana Vratas, in accordance with Sastric injunctions, one purifies himself. His body gets emancipated. The sins are destroyed. The Indriyas are controlled. The passion-nature of the mind gets subdued. This is Tapas. Contentment with whatsoever one obtains of its own accord without effort is Santosha. Astikya is firm, unshakable belief in the existence of God, in the words of the Guru, in the truths inculcated in the Vedas and the merits or demerits of actions stated in the Vedas. Dana is the distribution of money, cloth, food, grains, etc., earned lawfully at the sweat of the brow, with faith, to deserving persons without expectation of fruits and without the idea of agency. Isvara Pujana is the worshipping of Lord Hari, Siva, Krishna or Rama with

(32)

pure love, intense faith and single-minded devotion. Siddhanta Sravana is the enquiry into the right significance of Vedanta. It is the study and reflection of the nature of Brahman and the right significance of 'Tat Tvam Asi' Mahavakya. Hrih is the feeling of shame one experiences when he does certain actions which are not in accordance with the injunctions of the Vedas and rules of society. Mati is the faith in the paths prescribed by the Vedas for the attainment of God-consciousness or Self-realisation. Japa is the repetition of the Mantra into which one is duly initiated by the Guru or spiritual guide and which is not contrary to the rules of the Vedas. Vrata is the regular observance of or refraining from the actions prescribed or prohibited by the Vedas. The practice of Krichara, Chandrayana Vratas come under this heading. Krichara Vrata is fasting for 12 days. The observer of the Vrata drinks only some water. Many sins are destroyed by the practice of this Vrata.

2. Kriya Yoga

तपःस्वाध्यायेश्वरप्रणिधानानि क्रियायोगः । II-1

तपः mortification, स्वाध्याय study of scriptures, ईश्वर-प्रणिधानानि worship of God or self-surrender, क्रियायोगः the Yoga of purification.

Mortification, study of scriptures, self-surrender are the Yoga of purificatory action.

NOTES

In the previous Sutra, Saucha, Santosha, Tapas, Svadhyaya and Isvarapranidhana are described under Niyama. Here in this Sutra, three observances of the five are taken under the heading "Kriya Yoga." Every one of the item will be considered separately in the subsequent Sutras.

3. Benefits of Purification

समाधिभावनार्थः क्लेशतनूकरणार्थश्च । II-2

समाधि superconscious state, भावनार्थ for acquiring or bringing about, क्लेश afflictions, तनूकरणार्थः for attenuating, च and.

(Kriya Yoga is practised) for acquiring Samadhi and for attenuating the afflictions.

NOTES

The practice of Tapas, Svadhyaya and Isvara-pranidhana are intended to attenuate the afflictions and for preparing the mind for entering into Samadhi. They are for the purpose of purifying the mind of its impurities and for destroying distractions.

Purification is of two kinds. They are internal (mental) and external (physical). Mental purity is more important. Physical purity is also needed. Cleanliness is next to godliness. Physical, external purity alone is of no value. Much time must not be wasted in attending to external washing. By so doing, you forget the eternally pure Atman. The afflictions of the mind mentioned in this Sutra are described under Sutra II-3.

4. Benefits of External Purification

शौचात् स्वाङ्गजुगुप्सा परैरसंसर्गः । II-40

शौचात् by the purification, स्वाङ्ग for one's own body, जुगुप्सा disgust, परैः with others, असंसर्गः cessation of contact, not associating.

By the purification, comes disgust for one's own body and cessation of contact with others.

NOTES

The purity referred to here is physical or external purity. When the body is impure, one purifies it. Again it gets impure. Again he purifies it. He wants to keep the

body always pure but it constantly gets impure. Gradually
he gets disgust over the body which is full of impurities.
Since the same dust and impurity is in the body of others,
he ceases contact with others. Slowly the body idea drops
as he always thinks of the ever pure Atman. Moha and
Mamata for the body vanish. Lust disappears. The next
Sutra refers to the benefits of the internal purification.

5. Benefits of Internal Purification

सत्त्वशुद्धिसौमनस्यैकाग्र्येन्द्रियजयाऽत्मदर्शन-
योग्यत्वानि च । II-41

सत्त्वशुद्धि on the purity of Sattva, सौमनस्य cheerfulness of
mind, एकाग्र्य one-pointedness of mind, इन्द्रियजय conquest of
the organs or senses, आत्मदर्शन realisation of the Atman,
योग्यत्व fitness, च and.

**On the purity of Sattva, arise cheerfulness of mind,
conquest of the senses or organs, and fitness for the
realisation of the Atman.**

NOTES

The fruits of mental purity are described here. The
mind becomes Antarmukha, inward, as a result of the
conquest of senses. As the distractions drop away, there is
concentration of mind. By getting Antar Saucha, the mind
becomes fit for the realisation of Atman. Increase in Sattva
causes cheerfulness. Tamas produces gloom. If there is
always cheerfulness, remember that you are progressing in
Yoga. This is an important sign of spiritual growth. Many
Yogic practitioners put on 'Sunday faces' or castor oil faces
when they come outside to give interview to the visitors.
They are under delusion that people will take them for
advanced Yogis. There must be always joy and smile in the
face of Yogis. Then only they can radiate joy to others. Sri
Ramanuja also puts down cheerfulness as an important
measure for developing Bhakti. Joy is the very essence of
Purusha. In the Gita (XIV-2) you will find: "When the

wisdom light streameth forth from all gates of the body, then it may be known that Sattva is increasing." Prakasha on the face is Santosha. The means for getting Santosha is given in the next Sutra.

6. Santosha

सन्तोषादनुत्तमः सुखलाभः । II-42

सन्तोषाद् by contentment, अनुत्तमः supreme, सुख happiness, लाभः gained, obtained.

Supreme happiness is obtained through contentment.

NOTES

You will find in Yoga Vasishtha that Santosha, Santi, Vichara and Satsanga are the four sentinels at the door of Moksha. If you have Santosha, the other three will come by themselves. Santosha, contentment, is one of the important virtues for an aspirant. Riches and poverty are not counted by the amount of wealth one keeps. A king, if he keeps too many desires and if he wants more, is considered to be a beggar. A beggar, if he is contented with what he has, is really a king. From contentment comes real happiness. If a man has no contentment, his mind will be always wandering. It will be impossible to do concentration and other Yogic practices. Therefore contentment should be developed by all aspirants.

7. Tapas

कायेन्द्रियसिद्धिरशुद्धिक्षयात्तपसः । II-43

काय the physical body, इन्द्रिय senses, सिद्धि occult powers, अशुद्धि impurity, क्षयात् due to destruction, तपसः through mortification.

Through Tapas, mortification, due to the destruction of impurities, arise psychic powers in the body and senses.

NOTES

By Tapas, the mind, speech and Indriyas are purified.

Fasts and all religious observances that are laid down in Dharma Sastras and the rules of Yama and Niyama, Asana, Pranayama, etc., come under Tapas. In Gita Chapter XVII, the three Slokas from 14 to 16 describe three kinds of Tapas, viz., Tapas of body, speech and mind. Psychic powers are the eight Siddhis, Anima, Mahima, etc. All these Siddhis can be acquired by the steady practice of Tapas. Manu says: "He whose speech and mind are pure and ever carefully guarded, obtains all the fruits that are obtained by means of Vedanta." By the performance of Tapas, all Klesas (afflictions) and impurities can be destroyed.

8. Svadhyaya

स्वाध्यायादिष्टदेवतासम्प्रयोगः । II-44

स्वाध्यायाद् by study of scriptures, इष्टदेवता tutelary deity, सम्प्रयोगः communion.

By study of scriptures comes the communion with the tutelary deity.

NOTES

Svadhyaya is the study of scriptures such as the Gita, the Upanishads, the Ramayana, the Bhagavata, etc. The study should be done with concentration. You should understand what you have studied and try to put in your everyday life all that you have learnt. There will be no benefit in your study, if you do not exert to live up to the teachings of the scriptures. Svadhyaya includes also Japa, the repetition of Mantras. By constant study and its practice in daily life will lead one to have communion with God.

9. Isvarapranidhana

समाधिसिद्धिरीश्वरप्रणिधानात् । II-45

समाधि superconscious state, सिद्धि attainment, ईश्वरप्रणिधानात् by self-surrender.

By self-surrender comes attainment of Samadhi, superconscious state.

NOTES

The self-surrender should be free, perfect, unconditioned and ungrudging. Then the Samadhi will come by itself. This Pranidhana is further dealt with in Sutra I-23.

CHAPTER V

BHAKTI IN YOGA

1. Who Is Isvara

क्लेशकर्मविपाकाशयैरपरामृष्टः पुरुषविशेष ईश्वरः । I-24

क्लेश afflictions, कर्म works, विपाक fruition, आशयैः vehicles, अपरामृष्टः unaffected by, पुरुषविशेष particular soul, ईश्वरः God.

God is a particular soul unaffected by afflictions, works, fruition and vehicles.

NOTES

Yoga of Patanjali Maharshi is a complement of Sankhya philosophy of Kapila. Kapila denies the existence of an Isvara. He says that Prakriti can do everything. Patanjali Maharshi admits the existence an Isvara. This philosophy hence derives its significant name Sa-Isvara Sankhya. Isvara of Patanjali is neither the personal God of the Bhaktas nor the impersonal Brahman of the Vedantins. His God is a peculiar Purusha, completely free from all afflictions, works, fruition and vehicles.

2. Source of Knowledge

तत्र निरतिशयं सर्वज्ञबीजम् । I-25

तत्र in Him, निरतिशयम् the highest limit, सर्वज्ञ omniscience, बीजम् seed.

In Him is the highest limit of the seed of omniscience.

NOTES

The nature if Isvara is described in Sutras 24, 25 and 26. The way to develop devotion for Isvara is described in the Sutras 27 and 28. The fruits of devotion are described in Sutra 29. Infinite knowledge is God. Vayu Purana says:

"Omniscience, eternal satisfaction, eternal knowledge, independence, non-decreasing power, infinite power — these six are said to be the Angas of the Great Lord." Knowledge, non-attachment, Aisvarya, Tapas, truth, forgiveness, Dhairya or endurance, power of endurance, Atma Svarupajnana or knowledge of the Self and being the Adhishthana or substratum for everything and of all activities — these are the ten unchangeable (Avyayas) qualities that always exist in God.

3. The Guru of All

स पूर्वेषामपि गुरुः कालेनाऽनवच्छेदात् । I-26

स He (Isvara), पूर्वेषामपि of even the ancients, गुरुः teacher, कालेना time, अनवच्छेदात् not conditioned by.

He (God), being unconditioned by time, is the teacher of even the ancients.

NOTES

The ancient teachers were conditioned by time. But this Isvara is Adi-Guru, who is not conditioned by time. The magazine of knowledge and power is within. The help of a Guru is very necessary to awaken this knowledge. No spiritual progress is possible without the aid of a Guru. That Guru who removes the veil of aspirants and obstacles and throws light on their path, who is omniscient, who exists in the past, present and future, who is independent is God or Isvara.

4. Name of Isvara

तस्य वाचकः प्रणवः । I-27

तस्य Him (Isvara), वाचकः connotes, प्रणवः the sacred syllable Om.

The sacred syllable Om connotes Him (Isvara).

NOTES

Study Mandukya Upanishad. You will have a detailed,

elaborate explanation of this sacred syllable Om. Om is everything. In the Bible you will find: "In the beginning there was the word; the word was with God. The word itself is God." This word is Om. This world and the Vedas take their origin from Om. In the Gita you will find: "Om, the one-syllabled Brahman, reciting, thinking upon Me, he who goeth forth, abandoning the body, he goeth on the highest path." Lord Krishna says: "I am Omkara. I am Pranava in all Vedas. Of speech, I am Ekakshara, the one-syllable." In the Upanishads you will find: "Om is the bow; the mind is the arrow. Brahman is the target; know this Brahman with concentration; hit the target with Ekagrata; just as the arrow becomes one with the target, the individual soul will become identical with Brahman." Om has got four feet: Akara, Ukara, Makara and Ardhamatra; representing Visva, Taijasa, Prajna and Turiya.

A Sankalpa arose in Brahman. He wished: "May I become many." The physical vibration of Om in the physical plane corresponds to the original vibration in God when Srishti began. All the trinities, Sattva, Rajas and Tamas; Brahma, Vishnu and Siva; preservation, creation and destruction; Jagrat, Svapna and Sushupti; A, U and M; etc., are contained in Om. The glory of Om cannot be adequately described.

The syllable Om is the most appropriate name of the Supreme Self. Just as a man is pleased when addressed by a name dear to him, so also God is pleased when this name Om is used. The greatness of this monosyllable is further proved by the fact of its being frequently used in the beginning and end of Japa, sacrifice and study of the Vedas. A Mantra has no life without Om. The first Mantra of the first chapter of the Chhandogya Upanishad is: "One ought to meditate upon the syllable Om."

Lord Yama says to Nachiketas: "The goal which all the Vedas uniformly extol, which all acts of Tapas speak of, and wishing for which men lead the life of celibacy, the life of a Brahmacharin, that goal I tell you briefly. It is this Om."

'Pranava' means that which is always new. Pranava is unchanging and eternal. The relation between Sabdha and its meaning is Parinama Nitya and not Kutastha Nitya. Purusha only is Kutastha Nitya. Parinama Nitya is changing eternal. Kutastha Nitya is unchanging eternal. There are three factors in the comprehension of a word, e.g., milk. (1) the word 'milk.' (2) the object 'milk' and (3) the idea of 'milk' in the mind. Languages are different in different countries, but the ideas are the same. Sound-symbols vary. The idea of water is the same in all persons, but the sound-symbols are different viz., water in English; Pani in Hindi; Jal in Bengali and so on. Om is the basis for all sounds. All languages emanate from Om. The sound 'Om' starts from Nabhi (navel) and ends by closing the lips. Amen is only a modification of Om. You analyse and dissect any word. You will find Om there. All sound-symbols are centered in Om. That is the reason why Om is recognised as a common name for God by all religionists. The vibrations of Om can blow up a big mountain. Such is the power of Om. Every word has a corresponding object in the world. All words emanate from Om. Therefore in Om the world exists; in Om it is dissolved in cosmic Pralaya; and in Om it subsists. Om is the highest flower or offering for God.

5. Japa of Om

तज्जपस्तदर्थभावनम् । I-28

तद् its, जपः repetition, तद् its, अर्थ meaning, भावनम् meditation.

Its repetition and its meditation with meaning (should be practised).

NOTES

The aspirant gets one-pointed mind by the repetition of

Om. Avarana and Vikshepa slowly vanish. Japa is of three kinds, viz., Vaikhari (verbal), when the Japa is done loudly; Upamsu (semi-verbal), when the Japa is done in a whisper or humming mild tone; and Manasic (mental), when the Japa is done through the mind without moving the lips. The fruits of Upamsu Japa are a thousand times more powerful than the Vaikhari Japa, and the fruits of Manasic Japa are a lakh of times more powerful than the Vaikhari Japa. Mental Japa can be kept up even during work. It continues automatically during sleep also through force of habit. Beginners should do Vaikhari and Upamsu Japa. The significance of Om must be remembered during Japa. This is very, very important. The relation of the word and its meaning is eternal.

The mind of the Yogi who constantly repeats the Pranava and habituates the mind to the constant remembrance of the idea it carries, becomes one-pointed. The mind feels bliss in the one Lord alone. God showers His blessings on the Yogi. He gets the fruit of Samadhi and Kaivalya. You must make the Bhavana or the understanding of the significance of Om enter the mind over and over again by constant practice until it becomes part and parcel or the very substance of the mental existence. The Japa of Om should always be accompanied by meditation on Isvara. Mere parrot-like repetition or gramophonic repetition will not produce the maximum benefits. It has its own effects. Om serves as a boat to cross this ocean of Samsara. Om is a good companion for the mind. Just as soap washes cloth, so also Om washes the impurities of the mind. If you eat oranges twelve times, the force of Samskara and Vasana is increased in the mind. The greater the force of the Samskara, the greater the force of the Vasana for orange. Repetition strengthens the force of habit. By constant repetition of Om or any other Mantra, the force of spiritual Samskaras is increased. This is a great asset for you in the spiritual path. It will not allow the mind to run into the old grooves of Vishaya Vasanas or old ruts for sensual things.

6. Benefits of Japa

ततः प्रत्यक्चेतनाधिगमोऽप्यन्तरायाभावश्च । I-29

ततः thence, प्रत्यक् individual, चेतन soul, अधिगमः cognition, अपि also, अन्तराय obstacles, अभावः removal, च and.

Thence comes the cognition of the individual soul and also the removal of the obstacles.

NOTES

Through the grace of Isvara, the Yogi will not get any disease. The divine grace will descend when one repeats Om and meditates on its meaning with concentration. Japa makes the mind inward (Antarmukha Vritti), and removes all physical and mental obstacles. As Om and Isvara are inseparable, fixing the mind on Om means fixing the mind on Isvara. Doing Japa on Om is the remembrance of Isvara.

7. Benefits of Devotion

ईश्वरप्रणिधानाद्वा । I-23

ईश्वर Isvara, प्रणिधानाद् devotion and self-surrender, वा or.

Or, by devotion and self-surrender to God.

NOTES

In Sutra 20 of Chapter I, it is stated that Asamprajnata Samadhi is obtained by "faith, energy, memory, meditation and discernment." Success in Samadhi is speedier for those who have intense Vairagya. This is given in Sutra 21. And now in this Sutra it is given: "Or by devotion and self-surrender to Isvara." That is, success is rapid in attaining Asamprajnata Samadhi by devotion to Isvara. The devotee should have total, ungrudging, unreserved self-surrender to Isvara. He should entirely depend upon Isvara. He should not keep any secret desire or egoism for his self-gratification. He should not expect any kind of reward, even admiration, gratitude, thanks, for his services. He should completely dedicate himself and all his actions to the will of the Supreme Being. This is Isvarapranidhana. It is true devotion.

8. Instructions on Bhakti

Five things are indispensably requisite in Bhakti Marga. Bhakti should be of a Nishkamya type. It should be Avyabhicharini also. It should be Sadat (continuous) like Taila Dhara (flow of oil). The aspirant should observe Sadachara (right conduct). He should be very serious and earnest in his devotional practices. Then only realisation of God will come very quickly.

No development of Bhakti is possible without Sadachara (right conduct). Just as a disease can be cured by medicine as well as by dietetic adjustment, so also realisation of God can be had by devotion and Sadachara. Bhakti is the medicine. Sadachara represents dietetic adjustment.

If you remove a fish out of water and place it on the shore, it will flutter with intense agony. It will be thirsting for re-entry into the water. If you keep a boy in the cold water of Ganga for a short time, he will be greatly agitated. He will shriek and yell out. He will be eager to come out of water. When the house of a man has caught fire, the owner of the house runs immediately to the municipal office to get the fire-brigade for extinguishing the fire. He takes immediate steps. If the aspirant has the same thirsting, the same feeling, the same earnestness or seriousness for realising God as the fish has for getting into the water, as the boy has for getting out of the water, and as the man whose house is on fire has for getting the fire-brigade, he will have realisation of God in this very second. There is no doubt of this. O aspirants! Be very serious and earnest in your devotional practices. Run now to the Lotus Feet of

the Lord. Those people who are not serious and earnest
about their devotional practices have lost this world on this
end and God on the other end. They are hanging in the air
with head downward like Trishanku. Pitiable indeed is
their lot!

What is Jnana? Just as you see the thread in cloth, clay
in pots and jars, gold in ornaments, iron in various kinds of
implements, wood in chairs, benches and stools, so also see
God or Atman in man, in every being. To feel that God is
seated in your heart and in the hearts of all: "Vaudevah
Sarvamithi" is Jnana. Bhakti, when it gets ripe, brings
Jnana. When Bhakti gets matured Jnana dawns by itself.
The fruit of Ananya Bhakti is Jnana. Bhakti is the seed or
the mother. Jnana is the fruit or the son.

Bhakti Yoga and Jnana Yoga are not incompatibles like
acids and alkalis. One can combine Ananya Bhakti
(one-pointed devotion) with Jnana Yoga. The fruit of
Bhakti Yoga is Jnana. Highest love (Para Bhakti) and
Jnana are one. Perfect knowledge is love. Perfect love is
knowledge. Sri Sankara, Advaita Kevala Jnani was a great
Bhakta of Lord Hari, Hara and Devi. Jnana Deva of
Alandi, a great Yogi, was a Bhakta of Lord Krishna. Lord
Chaitanya (Gauranga Maha Prabhu) of Bengal was a fine
Advaita Vedanta scholar, and yet he danced in streets and
market places, singing Hari's names. Appayya Dikshitar, a
famous Jnani of Adaipalam, author of Siddhanta Lesha
and various other Vedantic books, was a devotee of Lord
Siva. It behoves, therefore, that Bhakti can be combined
with much advantage with Jnana.

CHAPTER VI

ASANA

1. What Is Asana

स्थिरसुखमासनम् । II-46

स्थिर steady, firm, सुखम् pleasant, comfortable, आसनम् posture.

Asana is steady, comfortable posture.

NOTES

Patanjali Maharshi does not lay much stress on either Asanas or Pranayama. He has not mentioned about Kundalini also in any of the Sutras. Hatha Yogins have developed Asanas and Pranayama as a separate branch of Yoga later on. They pay much attention to Asanas and Pranayama to open the Kundalini. Hatha Yoga is a physical Yoga. Raja Yoga is a mental Yoga. Where Hatha Yoga ends, there Raja Yoga begins. Hatha Yoga and Raja Yoga cannot be separated. They are interdependent. Asana is the third Anga of Raja Yoga.

In Svetasvatara Upanishad (II-8), you will find: "Keeping the upper parts, the chest, neck and the head erect and equal to the other parts of the body, subduing within the heart the senses together with the mind, let the wise by the raft of Brahman cross over all the fearful torrents of the world." Again in the Gita (VI-13) it is mentioned: "Let him firmly hold his body, head, neck erect and still, gazing at the tip of his nose, and not looking around."

Greater emphasis is given in all the scriptures for keeping up the head, chest and body erect and steady. In

(47)

the beginning stages of practice of concentration and meditation, the Sadhakas are particular to see that the head, neck, chest and body are erect. But later on, after a few minutes, the body begins to shake. Whenever the body is tossed, the mind also is disturbed. The trunk also begins to form a curve even without the knowledge of the Sadhakas. To avoid this trouble, the Rishis of yore have formulated four Asanas, viz., Siddhasana, Padmasana, Svastikasana and Sukhasana for practising Pranayama and Dhyana. Of the four Asanas, Siddhasana and Padmasana are very, very useful.

Padmasana

Sit on the ground over a blanket or a seat made of Kusha grass or a deer skin or a tiger skin. Spread the legs forward. Slowly bring the right foot and keep it over the left thigh. Then bring the left foot and carefully place it over the right thigh. Keep the head, neck and the trunk erect. Keep the hands on the knees. Or you can make a finger-lock and keep the locked hands over the left ankle. This is very convenient for some persons. Or you can place the left hand over the left knee and right hand over the right knee, palms facing upwards and the index finger touching the middle portion of the thumb. This is Chinmudra. If this posture, Padmasana, is not suitable, you can take recourse to Siddhasana.

Siddhasana

Place one heel at the anus. Keep the other heel on the root of the generative organ. The feet or the legs should be so nicely arranged that the ankle joints should be in a line or touch each other. Hands can be placed as in Padmasana. This is Siddhasana. There are some other varieties in Siddhasana. Difference lies in keeping the heels. Refer to my book: "Yoga Asanas".

2. How to Get Asanajaya

प्रयत्नशैथिल्यानन्तसमापत्तिभ्याम् । II-47

प्रयत्न effort, practice, शैथिल्य mild and steady, अनन्त infinite, endless, समापत्तिभ्याम् (mind) transforming itself or meditation.

By mild and steady practice and meditation on the Infinite.

NOTES

When you meditate on the Infinite, the mind is taken away from the body. Asana will become quite steady. If the mind becomes steady, the body also will become steady. Some take the word "Ananta" as the great serpent with 1000 heads which upholds the earth. If you meditate on the great serpent, then also the Asana will become steady. In Sutra 25 of Chapter III, you will find that a man gets the strength of an elephant by contemplating on the elephant. By contemplating on Hanuman, one gets the power of Hanuman. In the same way, if you contemplate on the steady Ananta that holds the earth, you will get the steadiness in posture.

If you can sit firmly in one Asana, then you have attained Asanajaya, mastery over posture. You will have to practise this gradually. First start with half an hour and then gradually increase the period. In three months' steady, regular practice, one can attain Asanajaya. When the Asana becomes steady you will not feel the body at all. You will experience great pleasure. If you sit in a posture that is not comfortable, then you may feel pain and the mind gets disturbed. Therefore in the previous Sutra a comfortable posture is prescribed.

3. Benefits of Asana

ततो द्वन्द्वानभिघातः । II-48

ततो then (when Asanajaya is obtained), द्वन्द्व the pairs of
opposites, अनभिघातः free from the disturbance.

**Then (when Asanajaya is obtained), (the practitioner) is
free from the disturbance of the pairs of opposites.**

NOTES

The pairs of opposites are heat and cold, pleasure
and pain, etc., which constitute all our worldly
experiences. If you get mastery over one Asana, then
only you are fit for taking up lessons in Pranayama and
Dhyana.

Asana checks the wandering habits and removes
Rajas and cures many kinds of diseases. One can easily
concentrate and nicely meditate when the Asana has
become firm and steady.

4. Instructions on Asanas

When you sit on the posture, think: "I am as firm as
a rock. Nothing can shake me." Give these suggestions
to the mind a dozen times. Then the Asana will become
steady soon. You must become a living statue when you
sit for Dhyana. Then only you will be able to sit for
three hours or even more at a stretch.

If there is pain in the legs after some time, stretch
the legs and shampoo them for five minutes and again
sit on the Asana. When you advance, you will not
experience any pain. You will experience on the other
hand immense joy. Never change the Asana like
Padmasana for a few days and then Siddhasana for
another few days and so on. Stick to one particular
Asana and practise it regularly.

There are some other Asanas that are very useful
such as Sirshasana, Sarvangasana, Paschimottanasana,

Matsyendrasana, etc. Beginners should neglect all these because they are described in Hatha Yoga books. They are excellent Asanas for the preservation of good health and Brahmacharya. Without these two, viz., health and Brahmacharya, nothing can be done in the spiritual path. Students of Raja Yoga should have a steady and healthy mind. And so, the body also should be healthy and strong. These wonderful Asanas can be harmoniously combined up by Raja Yogic students also. I have seen many Sadhakas in a sickly condition with very poor physique and dilapidated constitution. They can simply close their eyes and sit like a statue. But they could not manipulate their minds in the proper direction and attain success in Raja Yoga. Since I have already published a separate volume on "Yoga Asanas," I will pass on to the next chapter.

CHAPTER VII

PRANAYAMA

1. What Is Pranayama

तस्मिन्सति श्वासप्रश्वासयोर्गतिविच्छेदः प्राणायामः । II-49

तस्मिन् that (Asana), सति being acquired, श्वास inspiration, प्रश्वासयोः expiration, गति movements, विच्छेदः cessation of, प्राणायामः Pranayama or control of breath.

That (Asanajaya) being acquired, follows Pranayama or the control of breath—the cessation of the movements of inspiration and expiration.

NOTES

Pranayama is said to be the union of Prana and Apana. Pranayama, in the language of Yoga, means the process by which we understand the secret of Prana and control it. He, who has grasped this Prana, has grasped the very core of cosmic life and activity. He who has conquered and controlled this very essence, has not only subjected his own body and mind, but every other body, mind and power in this universe. Thus, Pranayama or the control of Prana is that means by which the Yogin tries to realise in this little body the whole of cosmic life, and tries to attain perfection by getting all the powers in the universe. His various exercises and training are for this end. A comprehensive knowledge of Prana and its function is absolutely necessary for Pranayama. Here, I will give you a short description. For detailed information and different exercises, refer to my book "Science of Pranayama."

2. What Is Prana

"He who knows Prana knows the Vedas," is the important declaration of the Srutis. You will find in the

(52)

Vedanta Sutras, "For the same reason, breath is Brahman."
Prana is the sum total of all energy that is manifest in the
Universe. It is the sum total of all the forces of nature.
Heat, light, electricity, magnetism are all the
manifestations of Prana. All forces, all powers and Prana
spring from the fountain or common source — Atman.
Whatever you behold in this sense-world, whatever moves
or works or has life, is but an expression or manifestation
of Prana. The Prana is related to the mind and through
mind to the will and through will to the individual soul, and
through this to the Supreme Being. If you know how to
control the little waves of Prana working through the mind,
then the secret of subjugating universal Prana will be
known to you. That which moves the steam engine of a
train and a steamer, that which makes the aeroplane glide
in Akasa, that which causes the motion of breath in lungs,
that which is the very life of this breath itself is Prana.

Pranavadins or Hatha Yogins consider that
Prana-Tattva is very superior to Manas-Tattva, the
'mind-principle.' They say, Prana is present even when the
mind is absent during slumber. It is through the vibrations
of psychic Prana that the life of the mind is kept up and
thought is produced. You see, hear, talk, sense, think, feel,
will and know through the help of Prana. Prana is the very
essence of cosmic life, that subtle principle which evolves
the whole universe into its present form and which is
pushing it towards its ultimate goal. The Prana may be
defined as the finest vital force in everything which
becomes visible on the physical plane as motion and action
and on the mental plane as thought.

Though Antahkarana is one, yet it assumes four names,
viz., Manas, Buddhi, Chitta and Ahamkara according to
the different functions it performs. Likewise, though Prana
is one, it assumes five forms, viz., Prana, Apana, Samana,
Udana and Vyana according to the different functions it
performs. This is termed as Vritti Bheda. The principal

Prana is called Mukhya Prana. The function of Mukhya Prana is respiration; Apana does excretion; Udana does deglutition; Vyana performs circulation of blood; and Samana does digestion.

3. Yoga Nadis

Nadis are the astral tubes made up of astral matter that carry the subtle Prana. It is through these Nadis that the vital force of Pranic current moves. Since these are made up of subtle matter, these cannot be seen by the naked eyes. These Yoga Nadis are not ordinary nerves, arteries and veins that are known to Vaidya Sastra. The body is filled with innumerable number of Nadis that cannot be counted. Nadis play a vital part in this Yoga. These subtle tubes — Yoga Nadis — have influence in the physical body.

4. Chakras

Wherever there is an interlacing of several nerves, arteries and veins, that centre is called as "Plexus." Similarly there are plexuses or centres of vital forces in the Sukshma Nadis. These are called as Chakras or Padmas. All Nadis spring from Kanda. It is in the junction where the Sushumna Nadi is connected with the Muladhara Chakra. Of the innumerable Nadis, Ida, Pingala and Sushumna are the most important. Ida and Pingala Nadis are on the two sides of the spinal cord and Sushumna is within the spinal cord. Ida operates through the left nostril and Pingala through the right nostril. When the breath operates through Sushumna, the mind becomes steady. This steadiness of mind is termed "Unmani Avastha," the highest state in Raja Yoga. If you sit for meditation when Sushumna is operating, you will have wonderful meditation. When the Nadis are full of impurities, the breath cannot pass through the middle Nadi. So, one should practise Pranayama for the purification of Nadis.

5. Prana and Mind

The mind of a man can be made to transcend ordinary experience and exist on a plane higher than that of reason known as superconscious state of concentration and gets beyond the limit of concentration. He comes face to face with facts which ordinary consciousness cannot comprehend. This ought to be achieved by proper training and manipulation of the subtle forces of the body, so as to cause them to give an upward push to the mind in the higher regions. When the mind is so raised into the superconscious state of perception, it begins to act from there and experience higher facts and higher knowledge. Such is the ultimate object of Yoga. The control of the vibratory Prana, means to a Yogin, the kindling of the fire of Supreme Knowledge, the realisation of the Self.

6. Prana and Breath

That which travels in the nerves of the physical body is gross Prana. That which moves in astral tubes or Yoga Nadis of the astral body is subtle Prana or psychic Prana. Breath is an external effect or manifestation of gross Prana. There is intimate connection or close relationship between the gross Prana and subtle Prana. Otherwise Hatha Yoga is impossible. Just as the stoppage of the fly-wheel of an engine brings about the stoppage of all other wheels in a factory, so also, the control or stoppage of the external breath leads to the efficient stoppage or control of the whole gross and subtle Prana of the physical and mental factories. Hence Pranayama exercises are practised.

If mind and Prana cease to exist, then thought will not arise in any way. Both these are one only, like the flower and its odour or a sesamum seed and the oil in it. Prana and mind stand to one another in the relationship of the supporter and the supported. If either of them is slain, then the other also will cease to exist. The destruction of both will confer Moksha on all. "The function of mind belongs to Prana; from Prana or life proceeds all" (Chhandogya Upanishad V: 14 & 15). If Prana departs from the body, all functions of organs cease immediately.

7. Pranayama Exercises

बाह्याभ्यन्तरस्तम्भवृत्तिर्देशकालसंख्याभिः
परिदृष्टो दीर्घसूक्ष्मः । II-50

बाह्य external, अभ्यन्तर internal, स्तम्भ restraint or holding process, वृत्तिः manifestation, देश place, काल time, संख्या number, परिपृष्टः regulated, दीर्घ long, सूक्ष्म subtle.

Pranayama is of long duration or subtle according to the external and internal restraint or holding process regulated by place, time and number.

NOTES

Puraka, Rechaka and Kumbhaka vary according to place, time and number. The period of Kumbhaka must be gradually increased. Kumbhaka gives strength. If you want to increase the Kumbhaka for more than three minutes the help of a Yogic Guru by your side is very necessary. You can suspend the breath for 2 or 3 minutes without the help of anybody. This is quite sufficient for all persons for purifying the nerves and for steadying the mind and for purposes of health.

By place is meant the inside or outside the body and the particular length of the breath in the act. It is calculated by Yogis that the breath is respectively 12, 16, 4, 8 and 0 finger-breadths long according to the Tattvas Prithvi, Apas, Tejas, Vayu or Akasa. Time is the duration of these, which is counted by Matra: 12 Matras for Puraka, 48 Matras for Kumbhaka and 24 Matras for Rechaka. Matra means a measure or time-unit. Some take one second as one Matra. The time taken in making three rounds of the knee with the palm of the hand, neither very slowly nor quickly and snapping the fingers once, is called a Matra.

The twinkling of an eye is sometimes taken as one Matra by some. Time taken by one normal respiration is taken as one Matra. Time taken up in pronouncing the monosyllable OM is regarded as one Matra. This is very convenient for practice. Many Pranayama practitioners adopt this time unit in their practice.

Number refers to the number of times the Pranayama is done. One should do by gradual practice 80 times in the morning, 80 in the evening and 80 at night and 80 times at mid-night. When Prana comes under the control of the Yogi, it is called Pranajaya or conquest of Prana.

When the breath flows towards the left nostril, it is called Ida or Chandra Nadi; when it flows through the right nostril it is called Pingala or Surya Nadi; and when it flows through both nostrils, it is called Sushumna or Agni. Meditation is very conducive when Sushumna is operating. The breath flows for two hours in each nostril. This time is distributed as follows: Prithvi flows for 1½; Apas Tattva 1¼; Tejas 1; Vayu Tattva ¾; and Akasa Tattva for ½ Naligas. (2½ Naligas for one hour). If you read Svara Udhaya, you will understand these points fully.

In Patanjali Yoga Sutras there is a description of Kevala Kumbhaka in Sutra 51 of Chapter II. This is a very advanced course. One should practise from stage to stage, step by step for getting success in the advanced course. We have seen before, that, subtle Prana has intimate connection with the respiration. By regulating inhalation, exhalation and retention, one can understand and control the subtle Prana. For the regulation of respiration and for the practice of Kevala Kumbhaka, the following exercises will help the Sadhakas.

8. Preliminary Exercise

Sit on Padmasana or Siddhasana. Slowly inhale the air through both the nostrils without making any sound. Do not retain the breath. Immediately exhale the air very, very slowly. Repeat this process ten or twenty times both morning and evening. Practise this regularly for three months. Then you can attempt for the Sukha Purvaka exercise where there is retention of breath. Inhalation is termed as 'Puraka'. 'Rechaka' is exhalation and 'Kumbhaka' is retention of breath. Svasa refers to Puraka and Prasvasa refers to Rechaka. This is given in Sutra 49 of Chapter II.

9. Sukha Purvaka Pranayama
(Easy Comfortable Pranayama)

Sit on Padmasana or Siddhasana in your meditation room. Close the right nostril with the right thumb. Draw in air slowly through the left nostril. Now close the left nostril also with the little and ring fingers of the right hand. Retain the breath as long as you can comfortably do. Then exhale very, very slowly through the right nostril after removing the thumb. Now half the process is over.

Then draw in the air through the right nostril as soon as you can completely exhale. Retain the breath as long as you can after closing the right nostril and then exhale through the left nostril after removing the little and the ring fingers. These six processes constitute one Pranayama. To start with, do 10 Pranayamas in the morning and 10 in the evening. Gradually increase the number to 20 in each sitting. Gradually increase the period of Kumbhaka also. Have a Bhavana (mental attitude) that all the Daivi Sampat as mercy, love, forgiveness, Santi, joy, etc., are entering your system along with the inspired air and all the Asuri Sampat such as lust, anger, greed, etc., are being thrown out along with the exhaled air. Repeat OM or Gayatri mentally during Puraka, Kumbhaka and Rechaka. Hard-working Sadhakas can do 320 Kumbhakas in four sittings at the rate of 80 in each sitting. This Pranayama exercise removes all diseases, purifies the Nadis, steadies the mind in concentration, improves digestion, increases the digestive power, helps in maintaining Brahmacharya and enables one to attain Kevala Kumbhaka in due course of practice.

10. Kevala Kumbhaka

बाह्याभ्यन्तरविषयाऽक्षेपी चतुर्थः । II-51

बाह्य external, अभ्यन्तर internal, विषय position, आक्षेपी beyond, चतुर्थः fourth.

The fourth (Pranayama exercise) is going beyond the internal and external positions.

NOTES

In the previous Sutras, three kinds of Pranayama exercises are given, viz., internal, external and the period of suspension. In this Sutra the highest stage of Pranayama, i.e., going beyond internal (Puraka) and external (Rechaka), is given.

This exercise is Kevala Kumbhaka wherein is neither Puraka nor Rechaka. There is Kumbhaka only. This is for advanced Yogins. Kumbhaka is of two kinds, viz., Sahita and Kevala. That which is coupled with inhalation and exhalation is termed Sahita Kumbhaka, which is described in Sukha Purvaka. That which is devoid of Puraka and Rechaka is Kevala Kumbhaka. When you get mastery in Sahita, it is said: "When after giving up of inhalation and exhalation, one holds his breath with ease, it is Kevala (absolute) Kumbhaka." He attains the state of Raja Yoga. The practitioner attains perfection in Yoga.

11. Benefits of Pranayama

ततः क्षीयते प्रकाशावरणम् । II-52

ततः then, क्षीयते destroyed, प्रकाश light, आवरणम् the covering, the veil of ignorance.

Then the covering of the light is destroyed.

NOTES

The ignorance caused by the Karma covers the light of knowledge. By the practice of Pranayama this covering is destroyed by the development of concentration and knowledge. The next Sutra says that the power of concentration increases by Pranayama, as the distractions are removed thereby.

12. Mind Fit for Concentration

धारणासु च योग्यता मनसः । II-53

धारणासु for concentration, योग्यता fitness, मनसः mind.

The mind becomes fit for concentration.

NOTES

The mind becomes quite steady after Pranayama. It can be fixed at any point. By the practice of Pranayama, Rajas and Tamas which screen the light of Purusha are destroyed. Then the real nature of the Purusha is realised. There is no Tapas greater than Pranayama. It causes Chitta Suddhi, Nadi Suddhi and Mano Suddhi. Pranayama practice destroys the Karmas which hurl down man in various sorts of activities. Karmas also act as a screen that destroys the purity of intellect. Pranayama serves as a Prayaschitta (that which nullifies the effects of Karma) for all sorts of sins. It removes the Doshas in the body, Indriyas and mind. Pranayama practice steadies the mind. Vikshepa is destroyed. Mind gets Ekagrata state. Constant practice enables one to observe perfect Brahmacharya.

13. Hints on Pranayama Practice

1. In the early morning answer the calls of nature and then sit for the practice. Pranayama should be practised in a well-ventilated room. Pranayama requires deep concentration and attention. Do not keep anyone by your side.

2. Before the practice, clean the nostrils thoroughly.

When you finish the practice take a cup of milk after 10 minutes. Do not take bath immediately after Pranayama.

3. Some people twist the muscles of the face when they do Kumbhaka. It should be strictly avoided. It is a symptom to indicate that they are going beyond their capacity. Such people cannot have a regulated Rechaka, Puraka and Kumbhaka.

4. Pranayama can be performed just before Japa and meditation. It will make the body light and you will enjoy your meditation. The Asana should be steady when you practise Pranayama and Dhyana. Do not scratch the body every now and then during Pranayama practice.

5. In the beginning of practise you should observe some time-unit for doing Puraka, Kumbhaka and Rechaka. The ratio is 1 : 4 : 2. When you have advanced in the practice, you need not distract the mind in counting and keeping time-unit. The lungs will tell you when you have finished the required rounds.

6. Do not perform Pranayama till you are fatigued. Take a few normal breaths after some Pranayama. That will give you relief. Do not make any sound when you do Puraka and Rechaka.

7. You should not expect the benefits after doing it for 2 or 3 minutes only for a day or two. Regular, steady practice is needed for a long time.

8. Pranayama cannot bring about Manonasa (annihilation of mind). The Vrittis are quietened only temporarily. You should practise Dharana, Dhyana and Samadhi.

CHAPTER VIII

MIND

PART 1

MODIFICATIONS OF MIND

1. Modifications of Mind

वृत्तयः पञ्चतय्यः क्लिष्टाऽक्लिष्टाः । I-5

वृत्तयः mental modifications, पञ्चतय्यः five kinds, क्लिष्टाः painful, अक्लिष्टाः not painful.

The mental modifications are five kinds, (some) painful and (others) not painful.

NOTES

If you want to suppress the modifications, it is necessary for you to have a comprehensive understanding of these modifications. The painful Vrittis have to be controlled by the not-painful Vrittis, and these in turn have to be mastered by Para Vairagya or absolute non-attachment or dispassion or indifference to sensual enjoyments. The painful Vrittis are those which bring the afflictions and become the field for the growth of the vehicle of actions (Karmasaya). Vrittis that emanate from Rajas and Tamas are all painful ones. All Vrittis that proceed from Sattva Guna are not-painful ones. Through Vairagya and Abhyasa the painful Rajasic-tamasic Vrittis are to be controlled. Good Samskaras are generated by Vairagya and Abhyasa.

2. Five Modifications

प्रमाणविपर्ययविकल्पनिद्रास्मृतयः । I-6

प्रमाण right knowledge, विपर्यय wrong knowledge, विकल्प imagination, निद्रा sleep, स्मृतयः memory.

They (the modifications) are right knowledge, wrong knowledge, imagination, sleep and memory.

NOTES

All the above five kinds of modifications are dealt with in the subsequent five Sutras.

3. Pramana

प्रत्यक्षानुमानागमाः प्रमाणानि । I-7

प्रत्यक्ष direct perception, अनुमान inference, आगमाः testimony, प्रमाणानि right knowledge.

Right knowledge is direct perception or inference or testimony.

NOTES

Right knowledge is that which is unquestionably reliable and true. Right knowledge is right cognition. Wrong knowledge is misconception.

These Pramanas are helps or steps to attain knowledge of the Self. They are of no use for one who is resting in his own native divine glory. A full-blown Yogi depends on his own realisation for his knowledge. He is not in need of these proofs. An ordinary man depends on Pratyaksha only for his knowledge. A little advanced man depends on Pratyaksha and Anumana. A little more advanced man depends on these three proofs. Pratyaksha is that knowledge which is caused by the direct contact of any of the five senses of knowledge, viz., ear, eye, tongue, skin and nose with the objects of knowledge. Proofs are the right sources of knowledge. If there is no contradiction in your two perceptions, you can call it a proof or right condition. If there is contradiction, you begin to doubt at once. You see a river or mountain. You feel heat and cold. You taste an orange or a mango. These are all Pratyaksha Pramanas or direct cognitions. There cannot be any contradictions in these experiences.

If there is flood in a river, you infer that there ought to have been a heavy rain on the previous day. If you see smoke, you infer that there must be fire. These are all inferences. Inference is knowledge produced by a previous knowledge of the relation between a characteristic mark and the possessor of the mark. You see a clear sign and from that you come to the thing signified. You see a table and infer that the table ought to have been made by a carpenter. You see the external universe and thereby infer that there must be a Creator. This is inference.

Testimony, Apta Vakya, Agama Pramana and Sabdha Pramana are all synonymous terms. A competent person is an Apta. He has omniscience. He is a Seer or a Sage who has direct knowledge or Aparokshanubhuti. He will not reason anything. The whole book of inner knowledge or knowledge of the Self is revealed to him like Amalaka fruit in the hand. His words serve as direct authority. There can never be any mistake in his statement. His words are infallible. The highest testimony is the Veda (Agama), which has come out of the mouth of Isvara. An Apta is a Seer who has Self-realisation. All his words are gospel truths. He has derived super-intuitional knowledge beyond the senses through Asamprajnata Samadhi. His words will not contradict reasoning and past human experiences. Sankhyas also have three Pramanas like Raja Yogins. The Naiyayikas add Upamana (Analogy) to the above three. Vedantins have six proofs. In addition to the above three, they have Upamana, Anupalabdhi (non-presence) and Artha-patti (implication). These three come under the category of Anumana.

4. Viparyaya

विपर्ययो मिथ्याज्ञानमतद्रूपप्रतिष्ठम् । I-8

विपर्ययः wrong knowledge, मिथ्याज्ञानम् unreal knowledge, अतद् not its own, रूपम् form, प्रतिष्ठम् possessing.

Wrong knowledge is false perception whose real form is not of its own.

NOTES

The real Svarupa of one thing does not appear. A false form appears in its stead. I will give you a clear illustration. Mother-of-pearl is mistaken for silver. A post is taken for a man. A rope is mistaken for a snake. Viparyaya is wrong cognition brought about by some defect either in the object itself or in the means leading to it. Doubt is also included in this.

5. Vikalpa

शब्दज्ञानानुपाती वस्तुशून्यो विकल्पः । I-9

शब्द mere words, ज्ञान knowledge, अनुपाति followed in consequence, वस्तु reality, शून्यः nothing, destitute of, विकल्पः imagination.

Imagination follows from mere words which have nothing in reality.

NOTES

As instances of Vikalpa we have: 'horns of a hare', 'son of a barren woman', 'lotus in the sky', 'intelligence of Purusha', 'head of Rahu', etc. The difference between Vikalpa and Viparyaya lies in the fact that Vikalpa can hardly be removed by a careful observation of the object, as Viparyaya is. As soon as you closely observe, the notion of silver in the mother-of-pearl, or snake in the rope, disappears.

Mind havocs through the power of imagination. Imaginary fears of various sorts, exaggeration, concoction, mental dramatisation, building castles in the air, are all due to the power of imagination. Even a perfect man full of health has some imaginary disease or other due to the power of imagination of the mind. A man may have a little weakness or Dosha (fault). When he becomes your enemy, you at once exaggerate and magnify his weaknesses and Doshas. This is due to the power of imagination. Much energy is wasted on account of imaginary fears.

Whenever the minds of two friends are strained by ill-feelings, these minds begin to exaggerate and concoct things. Fault-finding nature increases. It is very difficult to get at the truth of the statements of these two broken friends with broken friendship. Their utterances are always coloured by their inner feelings. The power of imagination havocs now. Maya havocs through mind and its power of imagination. May peace be unto them. May there be sympathy and better understanding amongst them.

I shall explain to you the nature of 'mental dramatisation.' Mark the ways of the mind. During conversation with your friend the mind sometimes imagines in vain that it has hurt the feelings of your friend. It spends much of its energy in unnecessary feelings. You think: 'How can I see him tomorrow morning? He may be displeased with me.' Next morning when you meet him, nothing happens. Your friend starts a pleasant conversation and smiles. You are surprised. To your great astonishment the subject of talk takes quite a different turn altogether. A family man imagines when a severe epidemic of plague ravages: 'What shall I do if my wife develops plague and dies now? I have got six children.' This is vain imagination. Nothing happens. Sometimes when the train moves slowly on the Pamban bridge over the sea, near Ramesvaram, the mind imagines: 'If the bridge gives way now, what will become of me? I will be smashed to pieces.' A touch of fear creeps in. There are thousand and one ways of mental dramatisation like these. The power of imagination plays a vital part in mental dramatisation. To destroy Vikalpa, you must have right knowledge described in Sutra I-7.

6. Nidra

अभावप्रत्ययालम्बना वृत्तिर्निद्रा । I-10

अभाव nothingness, प्रत्यय cause, आलम्बना support, वृत्तिः modification of mind, निद्रा sleep.

Sleep is a modification of mind which has the cause of nothingness as its support.

NOTES

Sleep manifests when there is preponderance of Tamas, when Sattva and Rajas subside and when there is no knowledge of the external world. Ordinary people think that there is Vritti-sunya in sleep. It is not so. As there is memory in you when you wake up and as you say when you wake up, 'I slept soundly; I knew nothing,' there ought to have been a particular kind of subtle wave in the mind during sleep (Abhavarupa Vritti). It should not be understood that sleep is no transformation or Vritti of the mind. If it were so, the remembrance: 'I slept soundly,' would not follow on waking, for you never remember what you have not experienced. Sleep is a particular kind of Vritti. This must be controlled like other Vrittis if you want to enter into Samadhi.

7. Smriti

अनुभूतविषयासम्प्रमोषः स्मृतिः । I-11

अनुभूत perceived, विषय objects, असम्प्रमोषः not slipping away, स्मृतिः memory.

Memory is 'not slipping away' of the objects perceived.

NOTES

Remembrance is a function brought entirely by the residuum or impression due to former experience. The objects cognised do not slip away from the mind. They come back to the surface of the conscious mind through the influence of Samskaras that are imbedded in the subconscious mind. Knowledge produced by recollecting impressions of past experiences is memory. The above five kinds of Vrittis come under the three categories, pleasure, pain or Moha (delusion or infatuation or fascination). Pramana, Viparyaya and Vikalpa are enjoyed in waking state. The Vasanas of these three Vrittis are enjoyed in dream.

PART 2

AFFLICTIONS OF MIND

1. What Are the Afflictions

अविद्यास्मितारागद्वेषाभिनिवेशाः क्लेशाः । II-3

अविद्या ignorance, अस्मिता egoism, राग attachment, द्वेष hatred, अभिनिवेश clinging to life, क्लेशाः afflictions.

The afflictions are ignorance, egoism, attachment, hatred and clinging to life

NOTES

All these disorders ruffle the mind like physical malady. Therefore they are great impediments to meditation. They hang upon man and make the qualities firm. They raise Vrittis and bring about fructification of Karmas by coming to depend upon one another for mutual support. If you eradicate Abhinivesa, Raga and Dvesha currents will die. If you remove egoism, these two currents, like and dislike will vanish. The root for egoism, Raga, Dvesha and Abhinivesa is ignorance. If ignorance is destroyed by getting knowledge of Purusha through Samadhi, the other four Klesas will die by themselves. The Karmas are supported by afflictions and the afflictions are supported by Karmas. This is mutual support. This is a Chakrika or cycle like the analogy of the seed and the tree

(Bija-Vriksha Nyaya). These Klesas develop the Mahat Tattva, egoism and Tanmatras. These are the five ties that bind a man to the wheel of birth and death. The most important knot is ignorance (Hridaya Granthi). This is the fundamental cause. The other four Klesas are the effects of ignorance. Pain and sin are ignorance only. These manifest in those who have forgotten the true all-blissful and eternally pure nature of Purusha. All the above five kinds of afflictions are dealt with separately in the subsequent Sutras.

2. What Is Avidya

अविद्या क्षेत्रमुत्तरेषां प्रसुप्ततनुविच्छिन्नोदाराणाम् । II-4

अविद्या ignorance, क्षेत्रम् field, उत्तरेषां for those that follow, प्रसुप्त dormant, तनु thinned, विच्छिन्न overpowered, उदाराणाम् expanded condition.

Avidya (ignorance) is the field of those that follow, whether they be in a dormant, thinned out, overpowered or expanded condition.

NOTES

Ignorance is the field or source for the four Klesas, viz., Asmita, Raga, Dvesha and Abhinivesa. These four afflictions are only modifications or varieties of Avidya only. These afflictions have four stages. In Prasupta state, they are hidden or dormant like the tree in the seed. Videhas and Prakritilayas have got this state. In Tanu Avastha, they are in an attenuated condition like a thin thread. Yogins who do practice have got this state. They thin out one evil Vasana by developing the counter-current or contrary good Vasanas. Anger is thinned out by developing mercy, love and forgiveness. In Vicchinna, they are in an overpowered state for the time being. When the husband fights with his wife, the love Vritti in him is for the time being in an overpowered state. The hatred Vritti is operating during the quarrel. As soon as the fight subsides, the love Vritti will manifest again in him when the wife smiles and speaks kind, loving words. In Udhara state, the Klesas are very powerful. They operate with full force. Vicchinna Avastha and Udhara Avastha are present in worldly persons. They bind one to Samsara. He who has Tanu Avastha can control the afflictions. There is another state termed Dagdha Avastha wherein the Klesas are fried out like burnt seeds. This exists in a full-blown Yogi who is established in Asamprajnata Samadhi.

3. Avidya Explained

अनित्याशुचिदुःखानात्मसु नित्यशुचिसुखात्मख्यातिरविद्या । II-5

अनित्य non-eternal, अशुचि impure, दुःख pain, अनात्मन् not-self, नित्य eternal, शुचि pure, सुख happy, आत्मन् Self, ख्यातिः taking, अविद्या ignorance.

Ignorance is taking the non-eternal impure, painful, and not-self as the eternal, pure, happy and the Self or Atman.

NOTES

Ignorance causes Vipareetha Bhavana (perverted understanding), and the man is rendered blind by passion and various sorts of Raga. He is under intoxication. Ignorance clouds understanding. An ignorant man is a dead man while living. He is a living buried soul, despite his wealth, possession and university knowledge. To take a thing for what is not, is ignorance. It is not a privation of knowledge. It is a Bhava Vastu. It does not mean absence of knowledge. You mistake this perishable body of five elements and various impurities as the pure Self. You think that you are the body only and you have forgotten the real nature of Purusha. This is delusion. This is ignorance.

4. How to Remove Avidya

विवेकख्यातिरविप्लवा हानोपायः । II-26

विवेकख्यातिः discrimination, अविप्लवा undisturbed, continuous, हान removal, उपाय method.

The method for the removal of ignorance is the continuous practice of discrimination.

NOTES

Discrimination must be undisturbed. It must become habitual. There must not be any break even for a twinkling of an eye. When discrimination operates, you will have complete inner life in Purusha. All the outgoing tendencies of the mind will stop. The Indriyas will be calm. This practice of discrimination is the cause for destroying ignorance, the cause of the junction of Prakriti and Purusha, leading to various experiences. Discrimination remains shaky as long as false knowledge has not been completely removed.

5. What Is Egoism

दृग्दर्शनशक्त्योरेकात्मतेवास्मिता । II-6

दृग् the seer, दर्शन the instrument of seeing, शक्त्योः powers, एकात्मता identity, इव appearance, अस्मिता egoism.

Egoism is the appearance of the identification of the power of consciousness with the power of the instrument of seeing.

NOTES

Egoism is the identification of the Seer with the power of seeing. Drik, the Seer, is the Purusha. Darsana is the instrument of seeing. The instrument of seeing is Antahkarana. Purusha joins with the Antahkarana and appears as if he is one or blended with the Antahkarana. Purusha has the Abhimana of 'I' in the Anatma — Antahkarana. The Antahkarana is mistaken for the sentient Purusha or Atman. This is Asmita. When you get anger, pain, misery, contentment, etc., you associate yourself with the Vrittis and say: "I am angry. I am miserable. I am happy." When the Atman is associated with the Antahkarana, the experiences of objects take place. Separate yourself from the Vrittis and the Antahkarana and stand aloof as the witness in your original all-blissful nature. This is Kaivalya. The means for destroying this egoism is given in Sutra II-10.

6. What Is Raga

सुखानुशयी रागः । II-7

सुख pleasure, अनुशयी attraction to, रागः attachment.

Attachment is the attraction to pleasure.

NOTES

Through the memory of pleasure enjoyed previously, the attachment or desire that arises towards pleasure or the means of pleasure (Sukha Sadhana, i.e., objects) is Raga. The desire for 'thinking on pleasure' (Sukha Chintana), is included under Raga. Egoism is the root cause for Raga. This is the reason why Raga is described after egoism. When pleasure is remembered, attachment is proceeded by the remembrance of the pleasure in consequence of the enjoyment thereof. Wherever there is pleasure, there is Raga side by side. Why are you very much attached to your wife? Because you derive pleasure from her. You love money; you are attached to money, because you can get various objects that can give you pleasure, through money. Everyone of us is in search of happiness. But attempt to get happiness is made in the wrong direction, in external objects, in the lap of the mother, toys, books, in University degrees, in wife, in money, in son, in honour and power. There is something dearer than a son, there is something dearer than a wife, there is something dearer than wealth, there is something dearer than this Prana or life itself. That 'dearer something' is Atman or Purusha, who is hidden in our heart. The search should be made within by withdrawing the mind from the objects, by controlling the Indriyas, by practising Yama, Niyama, concentration, meditation and Samadhi. Refer to Sutra II-10 for the removal of this Raga.

7. What Is Dvesha

दुःखानुशयी द्वेषः । II-8

दुःख pain, अनुशयी repulsion, द्वेषः aversion.

Aversion is that which dwells on pain.

NOTES

Through memory of pain from experiences, aversion comes towards pain and objects that give pain. This is Dvesha. You try to get rid of objects that give pain. Man shuns pain and runs after pleasure in this world. No one teaches him to seek pleasure. The mind is born of Ananda. So, it runs after pleasure.

Dvesha is the root cause for human sufferings. Wars, splits, dissensions, sectarian quarrels, murders are due to Dvesha. Wherever there is Dvesha, there is jealousy side by side. Jealousy is the intimate companion of Dvesha. Jealousy is petty-mindedness. It is a great pity to find that the minds of even highly educated persons who preach on the platform are filled with jealousy and hatred, and petty-mindedness. What a shame! As they are intelligent, they devise cunning methods and plans to destroy others, to get the whole fame and respect for themselves. A petty-minded preacher sows the seed of discard, disharmony everywhere. He is a pest and a menace to the society. He is a man of all evil. There is no redeeming feature in him. He does more harm than good. This Dvesha, aversion, should be completely annihilated. The remedy is given in Sutra II-10.

8. What Is Abhinivesa

स्वरसवाही विदुषोऽपि तथारूढोऽभिनिवेशः । II-9

स्वरस by its own potency, वाहि flowing, विदुष-अपि even in the learned, तथारूढ all the same established, अभिनिवेशः strong desire for life or clinging to life.

Abhinivesa is the strong desire for life, supported by its own potency, established all the same even in the learned.

NOTES

In all living beings exists the self-benediction: "May I continue to exist. May I live on." This self-benediction cannot exist in him who has not experienced the nature of death. By this the experience of former life is inferred. The experience of death in the previous birth remains as a subtle Vasana in next birth that this should be separated from this body. This Vritti is Abhinivesa. This Vritti will not remain in a man who has no experience of death. We infer from this that there had been previous birth in a man, from his fear of death. Even worms have got fear of death. This fear of death exists in both the learned and the ignorant. This fear cannot be explained by Pratyaksha, inferential and Sabdha Pramanas. The fear is common in both the literate and the illiterate. The past experience of pain of death is there in your mind. Therefore you are afraid of death in this life. This is the reason for the strong desire for life.

9. How to Remove Raga, Dvesha and Abhinivesa

ते प्रतिप्रसवहेयाः सूक्ष्माः । II-10

ते they (the afflictions), प्रतिप्रसव opposite modifications, हेयाः are destroyed, सूक्ष्मः subtle state.

They (the afflictions) are to be destroyed when they are in subtle state by raising opposite modifications.

NOTES

Klesas have two states, gross and subtle. When they are in a state of Samskara, they are subtle. When the Yogi enters into Samadhi, these Klesas are burnt up like burnt seeds and are dissolved along with the mind in the Purusha through the fire of knowledge. Svaroopa-nasa of the mind takes place when the mind moves inward towards the Purusha and gets Laya (dissolution) in the Purusha during Asamprajnata Samadhi. By raising opposite currents or waves of thoughts, the subtle Samskaras of Klesas should be destroyed. Hatred ceases not by hatred but ceases by love. This is the method suggested in this Sutra. This is Pratipaksha Bhavana method. Habituate the mind to contraries. Do always virtuous actions. Develop Sattvic qualities. These good Samskaras will act as antidotes to the Samskaras of Klesas. The method of Pratipaksha Bhavana is described in Sutra II-34.

10. How to Remove Evil Thoughts

वितर्कबाधने प्रतिपक्षभावनम् । II-33

वितर्क improper thoughts, evil thoughts, बाधने when obstructed, प्रतिपक्षभावनम् contrary good thoughts.

When obstructed by improper or evil thoughts, take to thinking on the contrary good thoughts.

NOTES

This is a practical exercise for spiritual development. If lust troubles you when you are practising Brahmacharya, entertain counter divine thoughts. Think of the glory of Brahmacharya and its marvellous benefits and the troubles brought about by lust. If a desire arises to injure any one, think of love and its benefits. If the habit of telling lies again manifests, think of the advantages of speaking truth and disadvantages of uttering falsehood. In this way, you can remove all defects by developing counter virtues or habituating the mind to contraries.

11. What Is Pratipaksha Bhavana

वितर्का हिंसादयः कृतकारितानुमोदिता लोभक्रोधमोहपूर्वका मृदुमध्याधिमात्रा दुःखज्ञानानन्तफला इति प्रतिपक्षभावनम् । II-34

वितर्का evil thoughts, हिंसादयः injury etc., कृत done, कारित caused to be done, अनुमोदिताः approved of, लोभ covetousness, क्रोध anger, मोह delusion, पूर्वका preceded by or through, मृदु slight, मध्य middling, अधिमात्रा great, दुःख pain, अज्ञान ignorance, अनन्त infinite, फल fruit, इति thus, प्रतिपक्षभावनम् thinking on contrary good thoughts.

When evil thoughts such as injury, falsehood, etc., whether done, caused to be done or approved of through greed, anger or delusion, of slight, medium or great intensity and in infinite ignorance and misery, take to the method of thinking contrary good thoughts or habituate the mind to contraries.

NOTES

If you hurt another man, or cause another commit injury to others or even approve of another doing so, it is sinful. Action and reaction are equal and opposite. If you injure another, it is bound to react on you whether in this moment or at a future date. When thoughts of injury come to you, think of the benefits of non-injury. This is the method of Pratipaksha Bhavana.

If you entertain contrary thoughts, all evil thoughts that obstruct Yoga will die.

You may fail in your attempt twenty times, but slowly you will gain inner spiritual strength. If you send a strong current of anger towards another, it will harm your enemy and pass even to the corner of distant lands and pollute the atmosphere there and come back again to you and harm you.

For destroying the following evil Vrittis, raise the opposite good Vrittis given against each: —

1. Lust (Kama) ... Brahmacharya, Mumukshatva.
2. Anger (Krodha) ... Love, Kshama (forgiveness), Daya (Mercy), Maitri (friendship), Santi, Dhriti (patience), Ahimsa.
3. Pride (Mada) ... Humility (Namrata or Vinaya).

4. Greed (Lobha)	... Honesty, disinterestedness, generosity, Santosha (contentment), Aparigraha (non-covetousness).
5. Jealousy (Irshya)	... Nobility (Udarata), magnanimity, Mudita (complacency).
6. Delusion (Moha)	... Viveka (discrimination).
7. Vanity, Hypocrisy (Dambha)	... Simplicity.
8. Darpa (arrogance)	... Politeness, Hri (Modesty).
9. Cunningness (crookedness)	... Arjava (straightforwardness).
10. Harshness	... Mildness.
11. Attachment (Raga)	... Vairagya.
12. Insincerity (Asraddha)	... Sraddha (faith).
13. Chanchalatvam (Fickleness)	... Determination (Nischaya Vritti).

12. The Root of Afflictions

क्लेशमूलः कर्माशयो दृष्टादृष्टजन्मवेदनीयः । II-12

क्लेशमूलः the root of afflictions, कर्माशयः the impressions of works, दृष्ट visible (present), अदृष्ट unseen (future), जन्म births, वेदनीयः experienced.

The impressions of works have their root in afflictions, and are experienced in this life and in the unseen future births.

NOTES

Klesas are responsible for works. They goad a man to do works and thereby enjoy the fruits of his actions. Suppose you do a very charitable act in this birth. The impression of this act is imbedded in a subtle form in the subconscious mind. It will give you fruit either in this or in any future birth. The sum total of all Samskaras is called 'Asaya.' Samskaras and Vasanas coexist. These impressions become ripe for fruition either good or bad when it is their time. Karmas are Anaadi or beginningless. In the Gita, you will find: *"Gahana karmano gathi"* — mysterious is the path of action. The law of Karma is inscrutable. It is difficult to say what sort of Karmas will cause leprosy or epilepsy, whether the fruit that you enjoy now is the result of one Karma or a combination of several Karmas.

A powerful Karma, good or bad, may bring fruits in this very birth. All Karmas do not produce their results all at once, nor does one Karma succeed another. From the Sanchita Karma, accumulated works, a certain portion is taken out for being worked out or exhausted in one birth. This forms the Prarabdha or fructescent Karmas of the present life. The works that you do now, current works or Agami (Kriyamana) are added to the sumtotal of works, Sanchita. The granary store of a merchant represents Sanchita Karma. The things that are kept in his shop correspond to the Prarabdha. The things that are sold daily represent Agami Karma. This is a rough analogy to illustrate our point. Ripe Karmas produce fruits under proper circumstances. Intense Tapas brings fruits at once.

Nandikesvara, Visvamitra and Markandeya did lot of Tapas and enjoyed the fruits in the same birth. Nahusha attained the position of Indra on account of his good deeds in his previous birth; but he was transformed into a serpent in the same birth on account of his sinful deeds in the same birth. The law of Karma is inexorable.

13. The Effect of Afflictions

सति मूले तद्विपाको जात्यायुर्भोगाः । II-13

सति मूले if root exists, तद्विपाकः its fruitions, जाति class, आयुः life, भोगाः experience.

The root being there, its fruition comes through class, life and experience.

NOTES

The root means, the root in the form of Klesas or afflictions. The results of Karma are threefold. They are Jati or class or species, life and experience of pleasure or pain. If there are Klesas, then only you will enjoy the fruits of Karma. From this it is inferred that the Yogi who has destroyed the Klesas will not have the fruits of Karma. Just as the paddy loses its power of sprouting when the husk is removed, so also, the Karmas lose their power of bringing fruits when the Klesas (husk) are destroyed by the Yogi. The Yogi destroys the Klesas by getting discrimination between Prakriti and Purusha.

It is not that one action is the cause of one life only. As we see in our lives different sorts of experiences, happy and painful, we infer that many ripe Karmas amongst the accumulated Sanchita join together and bring one life. One important Karma will direct the course of this life. It will be the ruling factor of this life. Many small Karmas will bring sometimes pleasure and sometimes pain. If you do any action, the tendency to repeat such actions (or Vasanas to goad you to do similar actions) are formed. If the tendencies are good, you will have to increase them through Viveka or discrimination.

If the tendencies are bad you will have to restrain them through Vairagya. You must try to do virtuous actions. Jiva can do actions in the other worlds also to a small extent. But, generally Heaven or Svarga is a world for enjoyments only. This Mrityu Loka (world of mortals) only is Karma Bhumi or world of actions.

There are only three kinds of actions viz., white (virtuous), black (vicious) and white-black (mixed actions). The actions of a Sannyasi are neither white nor black. The impressions of white actions brought about by the practice of Kriya Yoga destroy the black ones which have not begun to fructify. White actions bring pleasure. Black actions bring pain.

14. Fruits of Afflictions

ते ह्लादपरितापफलाः पुण्यापुण्यहेतुत्वात् । II-14

ते they, ह्लाद pleasure, परिताप pain, फलाः fruits, पुण्य virtue, अपुण्य vice, हेतुत्वात् cause.

They (class, life and experience) have pleasure or pain as their fruit according to the cause, virtue or vice.

NOTES

In Sutra II-13, it is stated that the fruit of afflictions comes through class, life and experience. In this Sutra, class, life and experiences are denoted by the word 'they'. Virtuous and vicious actions cause class, life and experience. As soon as these three are formed, the experience of pleasure and pain takes place according to virtue or vice. Karma has its origin in afflictions. Fruition has its origin in Karma.

15. Destroy Afflictions

ध्यानहेयास्तद्वृत्तयः । II-11

ध्यान by meditation, हेयाः destroyed, तद्वृत्तयः their modifications (the afflictions of mind).

Their modifications (five afflictions of mind) are to be destroyed by meditation.

NOTES

In Sutra II-10, instruction is given to destroy the subtle form of Klesas which are in the form of Samskaras. Here the way to destroy the gross form of Klesas which are in the form of Vrittis is described. The gross dirt of a cloth is removed by applying fullers-earth. The fine dirt is removed by the application of soap. There may be traces of subtle dirt in the cloth so long as the cloth is not destroyed. Even

so, the gross dirt of the mind – 'Klesas' – is removed by
Kriya Yoga. The gross Vrittis are destroyed by meditation.
In Samadhi, even the subtle form of Klesas (Samskaras)
are destroyed along with the destruction of the mind.
Regular, systematic meditation is necessary. It must
become habitual.

16. Karma in Yogis

कर्माशुक्लाकृष्णं योगिनस्त्रिविधमितरेषाम् । IV-7

कर्म actions, अशुक्ल neither white, अकृष्णम् nor black,
योगिनः of a Yogi, त्रिविधम् three kinds, इतरेषाम् for others.

**Actions of a Yogi are neither white nor black; for others
they are of three kinds.**

NOTES

A Yogi is not affected by his Karmas, because, he has
no attachment. He is absolutely desireless. Karmas cannot
bind him. He works without expectation of any fruits for
his actions. He has reached perfection. He works for the
uplift of humanity. Yogis acquire no impressions from their
actions. White actions are virtuous actions. Black actions
are evil actions. Mixed actions are a mixture of good and
evil actions. For worldly persons actions are of the above
three kinds.

17. Karma and Environments

ततस्तद्विपाकानुगुणानामेवाभिव्यक्तिर्वासनानाम् । IV-8

ततः from these, तद्विपाक their fruition, अनुगुणानाम्
favourable environments, एव alone, अभिव्यक्तिः
manifestation, वासनानाम् desires.

**From these (3 kinds of Karmas), there is manifestation of
those desires alone for which the environments are favourable.**

NOTES

When one has taken the body of Deva, the desires and
Vasanas of a human being will be in abeyance for the time

being. Only those Vasanas of the Deva which are favourable for the suitable environments in which he lives will manifest. The animal desires and human desires will be checked when one has taken the body of a Deva. When the Deva takes again the body of an animal, the animal desires only will manifest at that time. The Samskaras and desires of a Deva will be under check for the time being. The impressions and desires for which the conditions are not favourable, will lie dormant till their time comes in for sprouting or expression.

18. Karmas in a Viveki

परिणामतापसंस्कारदुःखैर्गुणवृत्तिविरोधाच्च

दुःखमेव सर्वं विवेकिनः । II-15

परिणाम consequences, ताप anxiety, संस्कार impressions, दुःखैः painful, गुण Gunas, qualities, वृत्ति functioning, विरोधात् due to contradiction, च and, दुःखमेव painful indeed, सर्वं all, विवेकिनः the man of discrimination.

To the man of discrimination, all is painful indeed due to the consequences, anxiety and impressions, and also of the contradiction of the functioning of Gunas (qualities).

NOTES

Pleasure is in reality pain only. In the Gita you will find: "The delights that are contact-born, they are verily wombs of pain, for they have beginning and end, O Kaunteya, not in them may rejoice the wise." Pleasure is mixed with pain, sin and fear. Enjoyment increases the Trishna or thirsting for objects. Trishna gives pain. The mind becomes more restless by tasting sensual pleasure. There is fear of loss of happiness. Sensual pleasure is imaginary. It is mental creation. It is Bhranti-Sukha. It is no happiness at all. For a man of discrimination the happiness that is derived from Self-realisation through Asamprajnata Samadhi only is the everlasting, real bliss. The very experience of pleasure creates a desire for more.

Desires are endless. When the desires are not gratified, there is uneasiness, disappointment and misery. The anxiety that is caused in taking care of the objects of pleasure brings great pain. The impression that is left in the mind of pleasure creates desires through memory of pleasure and brings pain. Another cause for pain is the natural opposition which exists between the individual actions of the three qualities Sattva, Rajas and Tamas. Rajas brings tossing of mind and distraction. Tamas causes delusion, carelessness, laziness, etc. Therefore, everything brings pain for the discriminating. Enjoyment cannot bring satisfaction of desires. Just as ghee when poured over fire aggravates it, so also enjoyment augments the desires. Kamagni increases. Pain comes if the desired object is not attained. Even if the object is obtained, one gets pain if the Indriya is weak and cold as he is not able to enjoy. Can a multi-millionaire enjoy palatable, rich dishes if he suffers from pain in the stomach? Hatred comes towards persons who stand in the way of enjoyment. Too much enjoyment brings diseases. These are all pains from 'Parinama'. The Yogi is afraid of Vasanas and Samskaras that are created during enjoyment. This gives him more pain. A worldly man who has a gross, impure mind is not conscious of the pain.

19. Avoid Misery

हेयं दुःखमनागतम् । II-16

हेयम् avoidable, दुःखम् misery, pain, अनागतम् not yet come.

The misery that has not yet come should be avoided.

NOTES

The avoidable is only the future pain. The pain which has passed away has already been explained. That which is being experienced now cannot be the subject of consideration here. Just as in medicine, the nature of diseases, their symptoms, prognosis, diagnosis, therapeutics, methods of treatment, prophylaxis, convalescence, etc., are considered in the treatment of diseases, so also, here, the nature of misery, its cause, strength, source and the means to avert are to be investigated.

20. The Cause of Misery

द्रष्टृदृश्ययोः संयोगो हेयहेतुः । II-17

द्रष्टृ the Seer, दृश्ययोः of the seen, संयोगः junction, हेय avoidable, हेतुः cause.

The junction of the Seer and the seen is the cause of the pain which is to be avoided.

NOTES

The cause for misery is the connection between the Seer and the seen. As the Chaitanya Sakti of the Purusha enters the Buddhi, the Purusha, who is only a witness and an Udaseena appears as Drashta. Drishya constitute all objects that are seen and also the instrument Buddhi through which it is seen, Indriyas, elements, etc. Buddhi is very near to Purusha. It is very subtle. Purusha is ever free and full of bliss. When conjunction takes place between the Purusha and mind (Buddhi), it appears to feel pleasure and pain through Adhyasa or reflection. By this conjunction through ignorance, the body, mind, Indriyas and Buddhi are mistaken for the real Purusha. Buddhi by its close contact with the Purusha and as it is very subtle and as the Sakti of Purusha has magnetised the Buddhi, appears like Purusha, just as the reflection of sun in water appears similar to the real sun. This is called Chit-Jada Granthi in Vedanta. This Abheda-Bhranti is Avidya, the root cause for all miseries. Kaivalya comes when this delusion is removed. If the conjunction between Buddhi and Purusha is removed, all miseries will terminate.

21. Definition of "the Seen"

प्रकाशक्रियास्थितिशीलं भूतेन्द्रियात्मकं
भोगापवर्गार्थं दृश्यम् । II-18

प्रकाश illumination, क्रिया action, स्थिति position, शीलं darkness, भूत elements, इन्द्रिय senses, आत्मकम् consists of, भोग experience, अपवर्ग absolution, अर्थम् objects, दृश्यम् the seen.

The seen consists of the elements and the senses, is of the nature of illumination, action and darkness, and is for the purpose of experience (through enjoyment) and absolution.

NOTES

The Svarupa of the Drishya (seen) is described here. From Pradhana downwards to elements and their combinations, it is all Drishya. Illumination, action and darkness are the functions of the three qualities of Sattva, Rajas and Tamas. If Sattva increases, illumination manifests. If there is increase of Rajas, action increases. If there is increase in Tamas, there is more darkness, inertia. Mahat or Buddhi, Ahamkara, Manas, Tanmatras, the five Jnana Indriyas, the five Karma Indriyas and the five gross elements are all modifications or Parinama or Vikritis of Pradhana. The Prakriti takes the Purusha around this world and gives all sorts of enjoyments of this world for his experience and finally makes him free when he gets discrimination between the Purusha and Prakriti. The real Purusha is ever pure and free. He is an embodiment of Bliss, Peace and Knowledge. He is unchanging and immortal. He has no beginning, middle or end. He is unattached.

Get all experiences of this little world quickly. Do whatever you want to get experiences of this dream-world. But, cut the cycle of birth and death quickly in this very birth, nay in this very second. Now, or never. Never forget the goal, ideal and the centre. The experiences will teach you that there is no essence in this physical life. It is all pain. It is all a long dream. There is no real love in this world. You will know that love here is selfish, hypocritical, changing and decaying, and that knowledge of Purusha and Atman only, through Asamprajnata Samadhi, can give real, undecaying bliss and eternal peace and immortality. Prakriti, the elements and this world are your best teachers. Be grateful to them. Get out of the net spread by Maya quickly and realise the Self rapidly with courage and cheerfulness.

22. Ignorance Is the Cause

तस्य हेतुरविद्या । II-24

तस्य its, हेतुः cause, अविद्या ignorance.

Its cause is ignorance.

NOTES

'Its' means, the cause of the junction of the seer and sight, nature and sight, nature and Purusha. In the previous Sutra, the Svarupa of Samyoga and its effects are described. Here the cause of Samyoga is given. To blend or unite the Drashta and the Drishya as one, and to think of this 'I' is Avidya or Bhranti. The Jiva increases the Bhavana of 'I' and 'mine' by mistaking the Anatma body and mind as Atman. The mind, which is saturated with the Bhranti-Vasana, gets Laya in Pradhana during the deluge or cosmic Pralaya and comes back again during projection of this world. Destroy this ignorance. Give up identification with this body and mind. Rise above body and mind and realise the Purusha who is beyond cause and effect, and who is, therefore, Anaadi (beginningless), Ananta (endless) and Nirvikara (changeless). Apply yourself to Sadhana and realise the Purusha. Do not make any delay. The monkey-mind will upset you.

23. The Means for Kaivalya

तदभावात्संयोगाभावो हानं तद्दृशेः कैवल्यम् । II-25

तद् its (ignorance), अभावात् disappearance, संयोगाभावः
disappearance of the junction, हानम् removal, तद् that, दृशेः
of the seer, कैवल्यम् independence.

**The Kaivalya, independence of the Seer, is the removal of
the conjunction of the Seer and the seen by the disappearance
of ignorance.**

NOTES

When you understand fully that the Gunas have
nothing to do with the Purusha and that the Purusha is
ever free, ignorance vanishes and discrimination dawns.
Then and then alone you will attain the state of Kaivalya or
Moksha. The scientists try to understand the external
physical forces of nature and to control them by suitable
methods. The Raja Yogis attempt to control the internal
psychic forces of the mind. Physical forces are gross and
the inner mental forces are subtle. Those who have
controlled the mental forces can very easily control the
external physical forces.

PART 3
DESIRES

1. Consecutiveness in Desires

जातिदेशकालव्यवहितानामप्यानन्तर्यं
स्मृतिसंस्कारयोरेकरूपत्वात् । IV-9

जाति class, देश place, काल time, व्यवहितानाम् distinct,
separated, अपि though, अनन्तर्यम् consecutiveness, स्मृति
memory, संस्कारयोः impressions, एकरूपत्वात् same in
appearance, unity.

There is consecutiveness in desires even though separated

88

RAJA.YOGA

by class, place and time on account of the unity of memory and impressions.

NOTES

Death is similar to sleep. Birth is like waking from sleep. When you see a friend whom you saw forty years ago the events and occurances that took place long ago come back to your memory at once, and those that happened recently are held in check or abeyance. This is your experience in your daily life. The same law applies to Vasanas and different kinds of births. There is unity or identity in Samskaras and memory. Desire Samskaras will manifest as desires. Kriya Samskaras will manifest as actions. Jnana Samskaras will manifest as Smriti or knowledge. The suckling of a child and the act of swimming of a duckling—these instinctive acts are proofs of a memory which must be the result of their corresponding and inseparable impressions left by the same acts in a previous incarnation. There is continuity of Vasanas or impressions as cause and effect. Every act leaves Samskaras in the Chitta which cause memory. Memory in its turn leads to fresh actions and fresh impressions. This cycle or Chakrika goes on from eternity like the analogy of seed and tree. In a human body the Samskaras of various human bodies only will operate. The Samskaras that were produced through experiene in other kinds of bodies lie dormant. Therefore, the continuity of bodies, Samskaras and desires is kept up, though there is separation in species, time and space. The desires, ideas and feelings constantly change. Some of the old desires, ideas and feelings are constantly departing from their store-house, the mind, and new ones are replacing them. This constant change does not in any way interfere with the harmony of mental operations. Only some of the old desires, ideas and feelings depart. Those that remain, work in healthy cooperation and concord with the new arrivals. The new arrivals are strongly magnetised by the old ones.

They both work in harmony and this harmony retains the identity of the mental existence.

2. Desire Is Beginningless

तासामनादित्वं चाशिषो नित्यत्वात् । IV-10

तासाम् they (Vasanas, desires), अनादित्वम् beginningless, च and, आशिषः desire to live, नित्यत्वात् eternal.

They (the Vasanas, desires) are beginningless, as the desire to live is eternal.

NOTES

'They' refers to 'the desires.' Desires have no beginning and end. Every being has clinging to this physical life (Abhinivesa). This 'will to live' is eternal. Experiences also are without any beginning. Brahman is 'Anadi Anantam'. Maya is 'Anadi Santam'. Maya terminates for that person who has attained knowledge of Atman. You cannot think of a time when this feeling of 'Aham' or 'I' has not existed. This 'I' exists continuously without any interruption. From this we can very easily infer that there had been previous births for us. Mind is very subtle and all-pervading like ether.

How could there be fear of death and desire to avoid pain, in any being, who has only been born, if he has had no experience of liability to death, it being understood that desire to avoid anything is only caused by remembrance suffered in consequence thereof? Nothing which is inherent in anything stands in need of a cause. How should it be that a child, who has not experienced his liability to death in the present life, should, as he may be falling away from the mother's lap, begin to tremble and hold with his hands tightly the necklace hanging on her breast? How is it that such a child should experience the fear of death, which can only be caused by the memory of the pain consequent upon aversion to death, whose existence is inferred by the trembling of the child?

Some philosophers say that the size of the mind corresponds to the size of the body with which it is connected. It contracts and expands like a light placed in a jar or a house, as the case may be. This is wrong. The flame of the light neither increases nor decreases, neither contracts nor expands according to the space. So also, the Vrittis of the mind only contract or expand. The mind remains the same always. The mind, therefore, is all-pervading and subtle. The happiness of a baby which is inferred from smiles should be considered as proof of a previous life.

3. How to Destroy Desires

हेतुफलाश्रयालम्बनैः संगृहीतत्वादेषामभावे तदभावः । IV-11

हेतु cause, फल effect, आश्रय substratum, आलम्बन support, संगृहीतत्वात् being held together, एषाम् these, अभावे on disappearance, तद् these, अभावः disappearance.

Being held together by cause, effect, substratum and support, they (Vasanas) disappear on the disappearance of these (cause, effect).

NOTES

Vasanas produce actions. Actions strengthen the Vasanas. Vasanas and actions produce Samskaras in the Chitta. Samskaras again produce Vasanas, memory and action. This Pravaha is running from Anaadikala. Egoism and Raga-Dvesha are the causes for virtuous and vicious actions. The Asraya is the Chitta wherein Samskaras are lodged. Alambana are the objects. The contact of the senses with objects brings in fresh desires. If the cause, effect, support and objects are destroyed, all desires also will be doubtless destroyed. Dharma brings happiness. Adharma brings pain. The cause for desire is happiness. The cause for hatred is pain. Effort takes place by these. This effort is done by mind, speech and action. Through this effort you favour some and hurt others. Enjoyment is not possible without hurting others. Then again by these acts, virtue, vice, pleasure, pain and through these Raga, Dvesha are again developed. This Samsara is kept up by this six-spoked wheel. Avidya makes this wheel to revolve. This is the root cause for all Klesas. This is Hetu. Phala is Jati, life-period and Bhoga (enjoyment).

4. Mind Acts for the Purusha

तदसंख्येयवासनाभिश्चित्रमपि परार्थं संहत्यकारित्वात् । IV-24

तद् that, असंख्येयवासनाभिः countless desires, चित्तम् mind, अपि also, परार्थम् exists for another (the Purusha), संहत्यकारित्वात् as it acts in association.

The mind through its countless desires acts (for the enjoyment) of another (the Purusha), as it acts in association.

NOTES

Just as the body exists for the enjoyment of the Indriyas, just as the Indriyas exist for the enjoyment of the mind, so also the mind exists for the enjoyment of the Purusha. Just as the house which has assumed its shape as such, by various meterials being brought together, exists for the enjoyment of another, so also this compound mind exists for the enjoyment of the Purusha.

5. Desireless Mind

तत्र ध्यानजमनाशयम् । IV-6

तत्र of these (minds of different desires), ध्यानजम् born of meditation, अनाशयम् free from desires and impressions.

Of these, the mind born of meditation is free from desires and impressions.

NOTES

There cannot be any abode for desires or Raga-dvesha (attraction and repulsion) or Punya-apunya (virtue and sin) in the mind that is born of meditation. The other minds born of Tapas, Mantras or herbs, etc., will have abode for desire, Raga-dvesha, etc. The minds are fivefold according to the means resorted to. This is explained in Sutra IV-1.

PART 4
GUNAS

1. Time and Gunas

अतीतानागतं स्वरूपतोऽस्त्यध्वभेदाद्धर्माणाम् । IV-12

अतीत past, अनागतम् future, स्वरूपगतः real nature, अस्ति exists, अध्व in the condition, भेदात् difference, धर्माणाम् characteristics.

The past and the future exist in their real nature due to the difference in the condition of the characteristics or qualities.

NOTES

The objects have the three experiences of the changes of past, present and future. As the effect is contained in a subtle state in the cause itself, that which is in a state of Sankocha (contraction) attains Vikasa (state of expansion), just like the tree from the seed. Vastu exists always. The outer coverings change, according to the changes of coverings of Gunas or qualities. As Gunas change, difference in Bhava also occurs. Changes take place like a Pravaha or continuous current. The future is a manifestation which is to be. The past is the experience which has been experienced. The present is that which is in active operation. We have these three periods of time with reference to a marked indicative point. The seeds of everything exists in a subtle state. That is the reason why Samyama on the three Parinamas produces knowledge of the past, present and future (*vide* Sutra III-16).

2. Nature of Characteristics

ते व्यक्तसूक्ष्मा गुणात्मानः । IV-13

ते they (characteristics), व्यक्त manifest, सूक्ष्माः subtle, गुणात्मानः nature of Gunas, qualities.

They (the characteristics), whether manifest or subtle, are of the nature of Gunas, qualities.

NOTES

These characteristics are of the nature of the manifested, when they exist in the present and are of the nature of the subtle when they are passed into the past or yet unmanifested. They are all from Mahat down to any object of the nature of Gunas. The Gunas change every minute and produce the various phenomena of nature. Past and present are due to the different modes of manifestation of these Gunas, Sattva, Rajas and Tamas. The whole manifested universe is made up of these three Gunas. Modifications of these Gunas constitute all sorts of Sthavara-jangama (immovable and moving things). In truth, the world is only Gunas.

3. Reality of Things

परिणामैकत्वाद्वस्तुतत्त्वम् । IV-14

परिणाम modification, एकत्वात् unity or oneness, वस्तु things, तत्त्वम् reality.

The reality of things is the result of the unity of modifications.

NOTES

As one Guna is prominent and the other two are subordinate there is only one Parinama. When the Sattva Guna is predominating, and Rajas and Tamas are under subordination, the organs of knowledge are formed. When Rajas is preponderating and the Sattva and Tamas are under subordination, the organs of action are formed. Each of these modifications is always known as one.

The strong current of Vrittis of the mind will be directed along the virtuous path if Sattva is predominating in the mind. The man will be doing virtuous actions. If Rajas and Tamas predominate, the mental current and mental energy flow along a vicious path and the man will be doing vicious actions. Sattvic mental current will make you inward (Antarmukha) and take you to Kaivalya or Moksha. Rajasic and Tamasic currents will throw you down in Samsara.

Sattva, Rajas and Tamas are the three Gunas or qualities of the Chitta. Sattva is its inherent quality. Chitta is born of Sattva Guna. But when it mixes with Rajas and Tamas, all the worldly taints manifest. Sattva is purity, light or knowledge.

Rajas is passion or activity. Tamas is inertia or darkness. By checking Rajas and Tamas, you can increase the Sattva. When Sattva increases, the mind becomes steady like the flame of a lamp in a windless place. He who is Sattvic can do real concentration and meditation, and can enter into Samadhi easily. A Rajasic man loves power and objects of senses. A Tamasic man does vicious actions on account of ignorance. No quality can stand by itself. Sattva is mixed with Rajas and Tamas. When there is preponderance of Sattva, Rajas and Tamas are controlled. They lurk themselves for the time being. When there is preponderance of Rajas, Sattva and Tamas are controlled. When there is preponderance of Tamas, Sattva and Rajas are controlled. Your important duty is to increase Sattva and to control the senses and the mind. Other duties are secondary. A sensible man only can understand this point. When there is increase of Sattva, there is brightness and brilliance in the face, lightness in the body, joy, purity, strength, peace and illumination.

Intense Rajas takes a Sattvic turn. Dacoit Ratnakar became the sage Valmiki. Jagai and Madai, who were intensely Rajasic and who pelted stones on Lord Gauranga, became his first disciples.

4. Stages of Gunas

विशेषाविशेषलिङ्गमात्रालिङ्गानि गुणपर्वाणि । II-19

विशेष defined, अविशेष undefined, लिङ्गमात्र indicated, marked, अलिङ्गानि non-indicated, without marks, गुण qualities, पर्वाणि stages.

The stages of Gunas, qualities, are the defined, undefined, indicated and non-indicated.

NOTES

The Visesha Tattvas which are 16 in number are the effects of Ahamkara and the five Tanmatras. The Avisesha Tattvas which are six in number are the effects of Mahat Tattva. These six Avisesha Tattvas are called Prakriti-Vikriti, because they are the effects of Mahat and the causes for the 16 Visesha Tattvas. These are the producers and the produced. The Visesha are the produced only. As the Mahat gets dissolution in the Alinga (Pradhana), it bears the names Linga. Pradhana is Trigunasamyavastha, wherein the three Gunas exist in a state of equilibrium. Read Sutra I-45. Mahat is the effect of Pradhana. That is the first manifestation.

Mahat is the cause for Avisesha Tattvas, Ahamkara and Tanmatras. It is also a producer and the produced, the defined or specialised.

Tattvas (Visesha) get involved into the Avisesha (undefined). The Avisesha along with the Visesha get involved into Mahat (Linga). Then, Avisesha along with the Visesha gets involved into the Mahat (Linga). Then the Avisesha along with Mahat gets Laya into the Alinga or the Pradhana. Pradhana is the final state of latency of the phenomenal world. Purusha is above Prakriti. He is not material. He is not a compound and therefore, He is Immortal. Vedanta is only an amplification and fulfilment of Sankhya Philosophy.

5. Hints on Gunas

If Sattva predominates in the mind, thoughts of God, Brahma Vichara will manifest. This mind will be one-pointed. The meditative mood will come by itself without exertion.

In spiritual neophytes the Sattvic state of mind will not last for a long time. Rajas and Tamas will try to rush in. You will have to be very vigilant. You will have to watch the mind through thoughtful introspection. A Sattvic man will be ever God-loving, dispassionate and powerful.

A Rajasic man will be ever engaged in worldly activities. He wants to lord over the people. He has domineering attitude. He wants powers. He is much attached to wife, children and property. Rajahs, Pandits and rich people are full of Rajas.

Just as you squeeze out the tooth-paste from the collapsible tube, you will have to squeeze out all Rajas from this bodily tube and fill it with Sattva. Then you will become a Dhyana Yogi.

The doors or impurities of the mind—Rajas and Tamas, should be removed by heating the mind with the fire of Vairagya and Abhyasa. This is referred to in Sutra I-15 and 16.

By increasing the Sattvic modifications of the mind as Kshama, love, mercy, magnanimity, generosity, truthfulness, celibacy, you can destroy the Rajasic and Tamasic mental Vrittis.

Although mind is one, it passes into many conditions or states, as it is made up of three qualities or Gunas. All these qualities enter into a variety of combinations. The modifications or Vrittis of the mind also are various. Peace of mind is a Sattvic Vritti. Lust is a Rajasic Vritti. Laziness is a Tamasic Vritti.

PART 5

MYSTERIES OF MIND

1. Ways of Mind Differ

वस्तुसाम्ये चित्तभेदात्तयोर्विभक्तः पन्थाः । IV-15

वस्तु objects, साम्ये the same or similar, चित्त minds, भेदात्
according to difference, तयोः their (minds'), विभक्तः
different, पन्थाः the ways of mind.

Though objects are similar, the ways of mind are different according to the difference in minds.

NOTES

The minds are different. The way in which the objects
affect the mind, and the way in which the mind is affected
by them are entirely different. Desires also vary according
to different minds. One mind wants money. Another mind
wants power, name and fame. Another mind wants woman.
Another mind runs after knowledge and spiritual pursuits.
Different Bhavas are formed by different men with
reference to one and the same object on account of
previous Samskaras and difference in the degree of the
qualities Sattva, Rajas and Tamas in their minds.

2. Mind and Perception

न चैकचित्ततन्त्रं वस्तु तदप्रमाणकं तदा किं स्यात् । IV-16

न nor, च and, एक single, चित्त mind, तन्त्रम् dependent, वस्तु
objects, तद् by that, प्रमाणकम् to be cognised, किम् what, स्यात्
would become.

Nor are objects the dependent of a single mind. Because what would become of (objects) if (they are) not cognised by that mind?

NOTES

If an object were dependent upon the mind, then in
case the mind were restrained or attending to some other

object, the object would not be touched thereby, nor would
it come into objective relationship with any other mind. It
would not be cognised by any other mind. Will it cease to
exist at the time? Or coming into relationship again with
the mind whence would it come back to life? Whence is
the object produced? If from the perceiving agent, whether
it is one mind that produces the object or many? If one, the
existence of an object thought of in a moment preceding
the thought of another object, cannot be possible. This is
not the case; because even when my mind has stopped to
think of an object, it is quite possible for the mind of Mr.
Johnson or Mr. Alfred to think of the very same object at
any subsequent time. I can also recognise the very same
object when I again think of the same object. Therefore,
objects cannot be said to be the result of the cognising
agent. Further the parts of an object which are not in
contact with the mind would not exist. Thus there would be
no back, and how could then there be the front itself? For
this reason, the object is self-dependent and common to all
the Purushas. Mind also is self-dependent. Mind comes
into relationship with the Purusha. Perception is attained
by its contact with the Purusha.

3. Mind Is Coloured by Objects

तदुपरागापेक्षित्वाच्चित्तस्य वस्तु ज्ञाताज्ञातम् । IV-17

तद् thereby, उपराग colouring, अपेक्षित्वात् since required,
चित्तस्य by the mind, वस्तु objects, ज्ञात known, अज्ञातम्
unknown.

**Since the mind is required to be coloured thereby (by
objects), the objects are known or unknown.**

NOTES

Objects are like magnet. They attract the mind and
produce lust, anger, etc., in the mind. The mind by itself is
free from lust, anger, etc. The mind is like iron. The
objects colour the mind and induce Vikara and change.

Colouring of the mind is further explained in the theory of perception in Sutra IV-16.

4. Purusha Knows All Modifications

सदा ज्ञाताश्चित्तवृत्तयस्तत्प्रभोः पुरुषस्यापरिणामित्वात् । IV-18

सदा always, ज्ञाताः known, चित्तवृत्तयः modifications of mind, तत्प्रभो to its Lord, पुरुषस्य Purusha, अपरिणामित्वात् due to the unchanging nature.

The modifications of mind are always known to its Lord (Purusha), due to His unchanging nature.

NOTES

Mind is an instrument for the sensations of pleasure and pain. Its chief function is to grasp the Vishayas. Grasping of things means, mind becomes modified by assuming the forms of the objects. It attains Parinama. Purusha has no Parinama or change. Purusha is superior to mind. He is separate from mind. Hence He is called 'the Lord'. Purusha is the ever-present witness of the mind. If the Purusha also is of changing nature like mind, He will also share the same fate as that of objects. Purusha is not an object of Vishaya by the mind. The consciousness is never suspended nor modified even for a second. Therefore, the unchanging Purusha exists. The modifications of the mind are, therefore, always known to the Purusha, its Lord. By this the unchangeable nature of the Purusha is inferred.

5. Mind Is Not Self-luminous

न तत्स्वाभासं दृश्यत्वात् । IV-19

न not, तत् it (the mind), स्वाभासम् self-luminous, दृश्यत्वात् because it is the knowable.

The mind is not self-luminous, because it is the knowable.

NOTES

"The sun does not shine there, nor the moon nor stars,

nor the lightning; then what to speak of this little fire? It shines by Itself and illuminates every thing. Its light illuminates all these." (Katha Upanishad.)

Mind is Jada or insentient, but it appears to be luminous by contact with the Purusha or nearness to Purusha. The light of the Purusha is reflected on the mind, just as the reflection of sun is thrown in water. From the experiences: 'I am hungry, I am powerful, I am afraid, I am dull,' you can very well understand that mind has no self-luminosity. Purusha alone is self-luminous. Mind shines in borrowed light from the Purusha. This is explained in Sutra IV-22.

6. Mind Does One Thing at a Time

एकसमये चोभयानवधारणम् । IV-20

एकसमये at one time, च and, उभये two things, अनवधारणम् impossible to cognise.

It is impossible for the mind to cognise two things at one time.

NOTES

It would be impossible for any one to be conscious of both the mind and the object cognised by it at the same time. If the mind is self-luminous, it will be able to cognise two things at a time. If it hears something, it cannot see another thing. But the Purusha can cognise all at one and the same time. Therefore, the Purusha is self-luminous. He is Sarvajna (all-knowing).

A spark of light presents the appearance of a continuous circle of light if it is made to rotate rapidly. Even so, the mind, though it can attend to one thing at a time, either hearing, seeing or smelling, though it can admit one kind of sensation at a time, yet we are led to believe that it does several actions at a time, because, it moves from one object to another with tremendous velocity, so rapidly, that its successive attention and perception appear as a simultaneous activity.

Perception through the finite mind or cognition or experience takes place serially, and not simultaneously. Simultaneous knowledge can only be had in Nirvikalpa Samadhi where past and future are blended into the present. A Yogi only will have simultaneous knowledge. A man of the world with a finite mind can have knowledge in succession only. Though several objects may come in contact simultaneously with the different sense organs, yet the mind acts like a gate-keeper, who can admit only one person at a time in the gate. The mind can send only one kind of sensation at a time to the mental factory inside for the manufacture of a decent percept and nice concept.

7. Cognition by One Mind

चित्तान्तरदृश्ये बुद्धिबुद्धेरतिप्रसङ्गः स्मृतिसङ्करश्च । IV-21

चित्तान्तरदृश्ये if cognition be postulated by another mind, बुद्धिबुद्धेः the cognisers to know, अतिप्रसङ्गः too many, स्मृतिसङ्करः confusion of memory, च and.

If cognition is postulated by another mind, there would be too many cognisers to know and the result will be confusion of memory.

NOTES

If you assume that there is another mind which cognises this mind, then there must be another mind to cognise that one mind and so on, *ad infinitum*. There will be no end to such minds. The defect of *regressus ad infinitum* or Anavastha Dosha will crop up. Further there will be confusion of memory. The world's process will not go on smoothly. Under these circumstances, therefore, we are sure that there does exist the Lord of the mind, the Purusha, the witness of the mind.

8. Mind Shines by Borrowed Light

चितेरप्रतिसंक्रमायास्तदाकारापत्तौ स्वबुद्धिसंवेदनम् । IV-22

चितेः Consciousness, अप्रतिसंक्रमायाः Purusha being unchangeable, तद् its, आकारापत्तौ by taking the form of the Purusha, स्वबुद्धिसंवेदनम् it becomes conscious.

Consciousness becomes conscious by taking the form of unchangeable.

NOTES

When the reflection of Chaitanya falls on the mind, the mind also shines under borrowed light from the Purusha. This deluded mind thinks foolishly that it is itself Purusha. This is Ajnana, the root cause for human sufferings. The mind is magnetised by the Purusha. The mind borrows its light and power from the unchangeable Purusha.

9. Mind Understands Everything

द्रष्टृदृश्योपरक्तं चित्तं सर्वार्थम् । IV-23

द्रष्टृदृश्योपरक्तम् the mind being coloured by the Seer and the seen, चित्तम् mind, सर्वार्थम् understands everything.

The mind, being coloured by the Seer and the seen, understands everything.

NOTES

Just as the transparent crystal and the red flower that is placed in close contact with it, appear as one and the same, just as the iron rod that is placed in fire appears as fire (Tadatmya Sambhanda), just as water when mixed with milk appears as milk, so also, the mind and Purusha appear as one (as Abheba). The mind is under double influence. It is affected by the objects outside and it takes the form of those objects. It is influenced by the Purusha and is rendered capable of cognising. Therefore, the mind acquires all knowledge of object. It gets the understanding power by the influence of Purusha.

10. Transformation of Mind

एतेन भूतेन्द्रियेषु धर्मलक्षणावस्थापरिणामा व्याख्याताः । III-13

एतेन by this, भूत in elements, इन्द्रियेषु in organs, धर्म property, लक्षण character, अवस्था condition, परिणामा changes or transformations, व्याख्याताः described.

By these transformations of property (form), character (time), and condition in the elements (matter) and Indriyas (organs) are explained.

NOTES

Antahkarana is Dharmi. It has three Dharmas viz., Vyuttana, Nirodha and Ekagrata. When one Dharma is operating, the other one has passed and the third one is yet to come. With reference to the Antahkarana, the Dharma that operates at the present moment is Dharma Parinama. With reference to what has passed and to that which is yet to come, it is Lakshana Parinama. If the present Dharma increases or decreases, it is Avastha Parinama. Thus the three kinds of Parinama occur in the Bhutas and Indriyas also. The mind assumes various forms. This is one kind of Parinama with reference to form. When the change becomes manifest in relation to some time, past, present or future, it is called Lakshana Parinama. When after this the particular property ripens into maturity or decay, it is called Avastha Parinama. The mind passes into various states. It is also Avastha Parinama.

11. Dharmi Explained

शान्तोदिताव्यपदेश्यधर्मानुपाती धर्मी । III-14

शान्त latent, उदित rising, अव्यपदेश indescribable, धर्म characteristics, अनुपाती common, धर्मी the object characterised or substratum.

The substratum is that which is common to the latent, rising and indescribable.

NOTES

'Avyapadesya' means subtle or hidden; hence
indescribable. The properties which have once manifested
and passed into a calm state are 'Santa.' They have played
their part well. They will manifest at a future date. Those
that are operating at the present moment are 'active.'

12. Changes in Dharmas

क्रमान्यत्वं परिणामान्यत्वे हेतुः । III-15

क्रम succession, अन्यत्वम् distinctness, परिणाम modifications, हेतुः cause.

**The succession of changes (in Dharmas and Dharmi) is
the cause for the distinctness of modifications.**

NOTES

The modifications of lust, pleasure, pain and Pramanas
are Pratyaksha. Samadhi state, Nirodha, Vasanas, the
connections between the Cheshtas of body and mind, the
power of objects, Punya-apunya Dharmas, certain other
modifications of the mind are Paroksha only.

PART 6

CONTROL OF MIND

1. Control by Abhyasa and Vairagya

अभ्यासवैराग्याभ्यां तन्निरोधः । I-12

अभ्यास by practice, वैराग्याभ्याम् by non-attachment, तद्
their, निरोधः control.

**Their (the mental modifications) control is done by
practice and non-attachment.**

NOTES

Through Vairagya you will have to check the out-going
Vishaya Vrittis and through Abhyasa you will have to cut
the new spiritual path for the mind to move on. Vairagya

serves the part of an anicut on the river of Vishaya Vrittis. It forms a strong embankment. It does not allow the Vishaya Vrittis to pass outside. Vairagya removes Pratibandhas or obstacles. Abhyasa gives Kaivalya Moksha. Without Vrittis one cannot enjoy sensual objects, (Vaishaya-Vyavahara). If the Vrittis along with Samskaras are destroyed, Manonasa or annihilation of the mind follows.

Here is the gloss of Vyasa: "The stream of mind flows both ways; flows towards good and it flows towards evil. That which flows on to perfect independence, Kaivalya, down the plane of discriminative knowledge is named the stream of happiness. That which leads to rebirth and the flow down the plane of indiscrimination or ignorance, is the stream of sin. Among those, the flow towards objects is thinned by Vairagya or desirelessness; the flow of discrimination is rendered visible by habituating the mind to the experience of knowledge. Hence the suppression of the mental modification is dependent upon both."

2. What Is Abhyasa

तत्र स्थितौ यत्नोऽभ्यासः । I-13

तत्र of these, स्थितौ steadiness, यत्नः continuous effort, अभ्यासः practice.

Of these (Abhyasa and Vairagya), practice is the effort to secure steadiness of (the modifications of mind).

NOTES

The effort to restrain all the Vrittis of the mind and to make the mind steady like the jet of a lamp in a windless place is Abhyasa. To drive back the mind to its source — Hridaya Guha, and get it absorbed in Atman is Abhyasa. To make the mind inward and to destroy all its out-going tendencies is Abhyasa. And this practice should be done for a long time without any break and with perfect devotion. This is mentioned in Sutra I-14.

In this Sutra Abhyasa is explained. As for Vairagya, refer to Sutra I-15.

3. Control by Suppression of Vrittis

व्युत्थाननिरोधसंस्कारयोरभिभवप्रादुर्भावौ निरोधक्षणचित्तान्वयो
निरोधपरिणामः । III-9

व्युत्थान out-going, निरोध suppression, संस्कारयोः of the impressions, अभिभव disappear, प्रादुर्भावौ appear, क्षण moment, चित्त mind, अन्वयः conjunction, निरोध suppression, परिणामः modification.

The suppression of the modification of mind (the Nirodha Bhumi) is the junction with the moment of suppression, when the out-going impressions and impressions of suppression disappear and appear.

NOTES

In other words, we can say that, by the suppression of the out-going Vrittis of mind and the development of modifications of control, the mind rests firm in Nirodha Bhumi. This is Nirodha Parinama (modification of control).

The mind remains in its real, unmodified state. It is very difficult to understand this and the following four Sutras. You must clearly understand the Chapter on 'Samadhi.' Vyutthana means the mind goes outward. Here it means Samprajnata Samadhi. When compared with Asamprajnata Samadhi, Samprajnata Samadhi is outward. Samprajnata Samadhi itself is a distraction of the mind. The passage from the Samprajnata to Asamprajnata Samadhi is very difficult and critical process. It is a trying stage. The Yogi must be very, very vigilant. If one out-going Vritti is checked and controlled, that powerful Vritti which checks the out-going Vritti is itself a modification. This also must be controlled. The mind should become absolutely waveless before Asamprajnata Samadhi is attained.

4. Make the Suppression Steady

तस्य प्रशान्तवाहिता संस्कारात् । III-10

तस्य its, प्रशान्तवाहिता undisturbed flow, संस्कारात् by habit.

Its undisturbed flow becomes steady by habit (continuous practice).

NOTES

The controlling modifications (Nirodha Parinama) must arise so continuously as to become a regular habit. Habit will come only by continuous practice. Then alone Samadhi will come by itself.

5. Control Mind by Virtues

मैत्रीकरुणामुदितोपेक्षाणां सुखदुःखपुण्यापुण्यविषयाणां
भावनातश्चित्तप्रसादनम् । I-33

मैत्री friendliness, करुणा mercy, मुदिता gladness, उपेक्षाणाम् indifference, सुख happiness, दुःख pain, पुण्य virtue, अपुण्य vice, विषयाणाम् towards the subjects, भावनातः cultivating habits, चित्त प्रसादनम् peace of mind.

By cultivating the habits of friendliness (towards equals), mercy (towards inferiors), gladness (towards superiors), and indifference towards happiness, pain, virtues and vice, comes peace of mind.

NOTES

The best and easy way of keeping the mind in a state of equanimity or evenness, which is conducive to the attainment of Samadhi, is described here. Maitri and Karuna will eradicate hatred. Mudita will remove jealousy. Mercy softens the hard heart and removes the cruel, harsh nature. By this practice, anger, Abhimana, hatred, egoism, envy of various sorts will vanish. Rajas and Tamas will be removed. The mind will be filled with Sattva. The fickleness of the mind will disappear. Ekagrata state of mind will come in. The mind becomes pure.

Samadhi cannot come in a mind that is filled with
hatred, jealousy and anger. By the method of Pratipaksha
Bhavana, any good virtue can be developed.

6. Control Mind by Pranayama

प्रच्छर्दनविधारणाभ्यां वा प्राणस्य । I-34

प्रच्छर्दन exhalation, विधारणाभ्याम् by retention, वा or, प्राणस्य
of the breath.

Or by exhalation and retention of breath.

NOTES

In the previous Sutra it is stated that by developing
virtues you can control the mind. Here, in this Sutra,
another method of controlling the mind is given. All Vrittis
will cease by the practice of Pranayama. Rajas and Tamas
will be removed. The mind will become one-pointed. The
body becomes light. The mind will become calm. Different
exercises in Pranayama are given in Chapter VII of this
book.

7. Control Mind by Vedantic Method

Cut off daily the branches of Sankalpa from the tree of
Manas and ultimately destroy the tree of the mind at its
root completely. The cutting off of the branches is only
secondary. The eradication of the tree by the removal of
ego is the primary thing. Therefore, through virtuous
actions, if you destroy the idea 'I' which forms the very root
of the mind, then it will not spring up again. The Brahma
Jnana which enquires the true nature of 'I' is the fire which
destroys the mind. It is the Jnanagni referred to in the Gita
IV-37: "The fire of wisdom reduces all actions (and the
false 'I') to ashes."

"He who knows the receptacle (Ayatana) verily
becomes the receptacle of his people. Mind is verily the
receptacle (of all our knowledge)." (Chhandogya Upanishad V-i-5)

CHAPTER IX

PRATYAHARA

1. What Is Pratyahara

स्वविषयासम्प्रयोगे चित्तस्वरूपानुकार
इवेन्द्रियाणां प्रत्याहारः । II-54

स्वविषय with their own objects, असम्प्रयोगे do not associate, चित्तस्वरूप nature of the mind-stuff, अनुकार imitate, इव as it were, इन्द्रियाणाम् senses, प्रत्याहारः abstraction.

Pratyahara or abstraction is that by which the senses do not associate with their own objects and imitate, as it were, the nature of the mind-stuff (Chitta).

NOTES

Pratyahara is abstraction. It is the withdrawal of the Indriyas from the objects. The senses are assimilated in the mind which is rendered pure through the practice of Yama, Niyama and Pranayama. The mind becomes more calm now. The nature of the Indriyas is to have always connection with the objects. Where the vision is turned outward (Bahirmukha Vritti), the rush of fleeting events engages the mind. The outgoing energies of the mind begin to play. When they are obstructed by the practice of Pratyahara, the other course for them is to mix with the mind and to be absorbed in the mind. The mind will not assume any form of any object. Hitherto, the Indriyas were following the mind like the other bees which follow the queen bee. Just as the bees fly as the queen bee flies, and sit as it sits down, so also, the Indriyas become restrained as the mind is restrained.

Pratyahara itself is termed as Yoga, as it is the most important Anga in Yoga Sadhana. This is the fifth rung in

(109)

the Yogic ladder. The first four rungs deal with ethical training and purification of body, mind and Nadis. Now with Pratyahara, proper Yoga begins which eventually culminates in Dharana, Dhyana and Samadhi. Hence in Kathopanishad also in Part VI, Sloka 11, you will find: "That firm control of the senses, they regard as Yoga." Again in the same Upanishad it is stated in Part IV, Sloka 1: "The Self-existent created the senses outgoing, therefore, one sees outside and not the Atman within. Some intelligent man, with his senses turned away from their object, desirous of immortality, sees the Atman within."

2. Benefits of Pratyahara

ततः परमा वश्यतेन्द्रियाणाम् । II-55

ततः thence, परमावश्यता supreme mastery, इन्द्रियाणाम् the senses.

Thence (from the practice of Pratyahara), comes the supreme mastery over the senses.

NOTES

Yogins enjoy sound, etc., without Raga and Dvesha. Worldly persons enjoy with Raga and Dvesha. This is the difference. The Yogi, not becoming a slave of the Vishayas, enjoys as a master out of his own free will. The Yogi enjoys by remaining as Tatastha (quite indifferent) with Raga and Dvesha experiencing the effects viz., pleasure and pain. The Indriyas cannot grasp the objects even though they are placed before them. This is Indriya Jaya. There is a difference between control and supreme control. By controlling one Indriya alone, the other four will not come under your control. When the mind is rendered pure and one-pointed and when it is turned inwards towards the Purusha, then and then alone supreme control of all organs follows.

He who has practised Pratyahara can have good
concentration and meditation. His mind is always peaceful.
This demands patience and constant practice. It takes
some years before one is well-established in Pratyahara.
He who has mastery over Pratyahara will never complain
of Vikshepa or distraction of mind. He can sit in a place in
a busy city where four roads meet and meditate whenever
he likes. He does not want a cave for meditation. Just as
the tortoise draws in on all sides its limbs, so also, the Yogi
withdraws all his senses from the objects of sense through
the practice of Pratyahara. Pratyahara gives power to the
practitioner. When the Indriyas are withdrawn from the
objects, then you can fix the mind on a particular point. It
is Dharana or concentration which is dealt with in the next
chapter. Pratyahara and Dharana are interdependent. You
cannot practise one without the other.

CHAPTER X

DHARANA

1. What Is Dharana

देशबन्धश्चित्तस्य धारणा । III-1

देशबन्धः fixing on one place, चित्तस्य of the mind, धारणा concentration.

Dharana or concentration is the fixing the mind on one place (object or idea)

NOTES

Dharana is the fixing of the mind on something external or internal. The mind can be fixed externally on the picture of Lord Hari, Lord Krishna or Lord Rama or on any other object or point. Internally it can be fixed on any Chakra or any part of the body or on any abstract idea. Having controlled the Prana through Pranayama and the Indriyas through Pratyahara, you should try to fix the mind on something. In Dharana you will have only one Vritti or wave in the mind-lake. The mind assumes the form of only one object. All other operations of the mind are suspended or stopped. Different objects of Dharana and their effects are given in the subsequent lessons. According to the Hatha Yogic school, a Yogi who can suspend his breath by Kumbhaka for 20 minutes can have a very good Dharana. He will have tranquillity of mind. Pranayama steadies the mind, removes the Vikshepa and increases the power of concentration. Fixing the mind on something is Dharana or concentration of mind. Dharana can be done only if you are free from the distractions of mind.

(112)

2. The Mind of Distractions

वृत्तिसारूप्यमितरत्र । I-4

वृत्ति modification of mind, सारूप्यम् identification, इतरत्र at other times.

At other times (when there is no concentration), the seer has identification of the modifications of the mind.

NOTES

When the seer does not abide in his own native state, he connects himself with the various Vrittis. He becomes assimilated with transformations. If your son is seriously ailing, you identify yourself with the Vritti and get grief. You have forgotten your essential divine nature. The Vrittis that arise from the mind obscure your native state. They are like clouds that screen the sun. During the time of concentration, the seer identifies himself with his own native state. At other times of concentration, the seer identifies with his Vrittis. This is a great distraction of the mind. The remedy for the evil effects of distractions is suggested in Sutra 30 and 31 of Chapter I. Have a comprehensive understanding of these modifications of mind. The painful Vrittis have to be controlled by the not-painful Vrittis, and these in turn have to be mastered by Para Vairagya. The painful Vrittis are those which bring the afflictions and become the field for the growth of the afflictions and become the field for the growth of the vehicle of actions (Karmasaya). Vrittis that emanate from Rajas and Tamas are painful ones. Vrittis that arise from Sattva Guna are not painful ones. Through Vairagya and Abhyasa the painful Vrittis are to be controlled. Then concentration will become habitual. For practising Dharana different kinds of exercises are given in the subsequent pages.

3. Dharana on Sense Perception

विषयवती वा प्रवृत्तिरुत्पन्ना मनसः स्थितिनिबन्धिनी । I-35

विषयवती sense perception, वा or, प्रवृत्तिः by enjoyment of senses, उत्पन्ना brought about, मनसा of mind, स्थिति steadiness of mind, निबन्धिनी cause.

Or, the practice of concentration on higher sense perceptions brought about by the enjoyment of senses, causes steadiness of mind.

NOTES

In the previous Sutra, Pranayama practice is prescribed for steadying the wandering mind. In this Sutra it is stated: "Or by the practice of concentration."

By the term: "brought about by the enjoyment of senses" refers to the experiences or sense perceptions, such as smell, taste, sound, feeling, etc.

By concentrating on the tip of the nose, the Yogi experiences Divya Gandha; by concentrating on the tip of the tongue, he tastes Divya essences; by concentrating on the palate, the Yogi experiences Divya colour; by concentrating on the middle of the tongue, he experiences Divya touch; by concentrating at the root of the tongue, he experiences Divya sounds. By concentrating on these super-sensual perceptions, he gets steadiness of mind. These experiences give him definite encouragement. He gets faith in Yoga.

Then he applies himself with great intensity and diligence to Sadhana for getting higher experiences in Yoga by entering into Samadhi. By concentrating on the moon, sun, planets, jewels, lamp and precious stones, one can get higher super-sensual experiences and can reach Samadhi.

4. Dharana on Sattvic Mind

विशोका वा ज्योतिष्मती । I-36

विशोका sorrowless condition of the mind, वा or, ज्योतिष्मती full of light, luminous.

Or, by meditation on the sorrowless condition of mind or the luminous mind.

NOTES

The word 'or' means, here is another method for steadying the mind. For concentrating on the Sattvic mind, it is necessary to concentrate on the seat of the mind, viz., the heart. The description is given below.

There is a lotus with the face downwards below the heart with 8 petals. Inhale and throw the breath. This exhalation will turn the lotus with the petals upwards. Imagine also when you exhale that the lotus is turned upwards. Then meditate on the effulgent light that is inside the lotus. The Sushumna Nadi or Brahma-Nadi passes through this lotus. This is another method of concentration for steadying the mind and attaining Samadhi.

There is a special concentration on this lotus. You will have to locate the four parts of the Pranava A, U, M and Ardhamatra, the point in the lotus. In the centre of the lotus, there is the sphere of the sun, the seat of waking state with the letter A; above this, the sphere of the moon, the seat of dreaming state with the letter U; above this, sphere of fire, the seat of sleep with the letter M; above this, Chidakasa, the seat of Turiya, the state known as Brahma Nada, the fourth state, which the knowers of Brahman call half-measure or Ardha-matra. In the stalk thereof is the artery of Brahma (the Brahma-Nadi —Sushumna) with its face upwards. This passes through the spheres of the sun, etc. That is the seat of the mind. The Yogi concentrates at this centre.

5. Dharana on the Desireless Mind

वीतरागविषयं वा चित्तम् । I-37

वीतरागविषयम् free from desire for objects, वा or, चित्तम् mind.

Or, on the mind that is free from desire for objects.

NOTES

Meditate on the pure mind or heart of Mahatmas or great persons like Sri Vyasa, Sukha Deva, Sri Sankaracharya, Dattatreya, Janaka, Lord Jesus or Buddha. The absorption of the mind in another mind ever pure, steady and blissful will certainly cause corresponding effect and lead to Samadhi. If you find it difficult to practise this, adopt the following method.

6. Dharana on the Knowledge of Dream

स्वप्ननिद्राज्ञानालम्बनं वा । I-38

स्वप्न dream, निद्रा sound sleep, ज्ञान knowledge, आलम्बनम् the object of concentration, वा or.

Or, concentration on the knowledge of dream and sound sleep.

NOTES

Steadiness of the mind and Samadhi will follow by practising this method. Some times you get beautiful vision of Lord Siva, Krishna or Rama or various other deities or holy personages in dreams. When you wake up you get elated. You can concentrate and meditate on any such vision you get in dream. You can meditate on the blissful state of deep sleep or on the idea: "I slept happily." According to Yoga, sleep is not a mere blank. By the purity of mind and by the grace of the Lord, the Bhaktas get His Darshan in dream and sleep, and they get Mantras also for their Japa.

7. Dharana on Triputi

क्षीणवृत्तेरभिजातस्येव मणेर्ग्रहीतृग्रहणग्राह्येषु
तत्स्थतदञ्जनता समापत्तिः । I-41

क्षीण powerless, वृत्तेः modifications of the mind, अभिजातस्य pure or clear, इवमणेः crystal-like, ग्रहीतृ knower, ग्रहण knowable, ग्राह्य knowledge, तत्स्थ similar to the objects, तदञ्जनता similar to the colour of the object, समापत्तिः concentration.

The Yogi, whose mental modifications become powerless, whose mind is as clear as a crystal and having the power of appearing similar to the colour of the objects, obtains concentration of mind by meditating on the knower, knowable and knowledge.

NOTES

When all the Vrittis are controlled and when the mind is one-pointed, it is transparent like a crystal. The mind loses itself in the object concentrated upon. The mind acquires the power of appearing in the shape of whatever is presented to it, be it the knower, the knowable or the knowledge. Just as the crystal becomes coloured by the colour of the object placed before it and then shines according to the form of the object, so also this mind is coloured by the colour of the object presented to it, and then appears in the form of the object. 'Samapatti' is Tanmaya Parinama. The mind gets the quality of the object which it comes in contact with. This is Grahya-samapatti. This is the first state. If the mind leaves connection with objects, if it keeps connection with the Indriyas only, it is called Grahana-samapatti. Grahana means the Indriyas. This is the second state. If the mind keeps connection with the Atman only, it is called Grahitri-samapatti. Grahitri means: "He who knows." That is the Self. This is the third state.

The Sutra gives you the condition of the mind of

concentration. The Vrittis should be annihilated. The mind should be pure like a crystal and then concentrate on the knower, knowable and knowledge.

8. Dharana on Any Chosen Object

यथाभिमतध्यानाद्वा । I-39

यथाभिमत according to one's own choice, ध्यानात् by meditating, वा or.

Or by meditating on one's own chosen object.

NOTES

Meditate on anything that appeals to you good or anything which the mind likes best. Having suggested so many methods in the above Sutras for concentration, and meditation, Patanjali Maharshi in the end says: "Concentrate on any object that appeals to you much." You can select any pleasant object that brings in concentration of the mind easily. This is the meaning of this Sutra.

Select any gross object that the mind likes such as pencil, apple, rose, chair, etc., and concentrate on it. The mind should be trained to concentrate on gross forms and objects in the beginning period of Sadhana and then gradually it can concentrate on subtle objects. After a regular practice on these, the mind becomes fit for concentration on internal Chakras and abstract ideas. Retire into a solitary place. Sit in a steady posture. Close your eyes. Avoid all distractions. Then you will have wonderful concentration. When you concentrate on one object, do not think of any other object. In this chapter a few exercises are given for Dharana.

In the next Chapter 'Samyama,' various gross and subtle objects and centres in body are given. You must have a thorough study of the chapters: "Pratyahara, Dharana, Samyama, Dhyana and Samadhi." They are something like one subject. The exercise "Trataka—steady gazing," given in Shat Karmas (six purificatory actions) of Hatha Yoga, is also a kind of exercise in Dharana.

Vedantins try to fix their mind on Atman, the Inner Self. This is their Dharana. When Hatha Yogins concentrate their mind on Shat Chakras or the six centres of spiritual energy, they concentrate their mind on the respective presiding Devatas and Tattvas. Bhaktas concentrate their mind on their Ishta Devata. Dharana is an important stage for any kind of Sadhana. You can concentrate on the virtuous qualities of your father or great persons, saints or prophets. This is abstract concentration (Sukshma). Beginners can concentrate on the *tik-tik* sound of the watch. Hatha Yogins concentrate on a small black dot when they do Trataka. This is also very good for beginners. Trataka on the picture of Lord Krishna can be done by Bhaktas.

9. The Concentrated Mind

शान्तोदितौ तुल्यप्रत्ययौ चित्तस्यैकाग्रतापरिणामः । III 12

शान्तोदितौ the subsiding and rising (the past and the present), तुल्यप्रत्ययौ having similar acts, चित्तस्य of the mind, एकाग्रता one-pointed concentration, परिणामः modification.

The one-pointed modification of the mind (concentration), comes when the subsiding and rising (the past and the present) are rendered similar.

NOTES

Sometimes when you are deeply engrossed in a subject you do not know how the time has passed. You say, "Is it 12 o'clock now? How the time has passed! I sat at six in the morning. It is twelve now. I have not taken even my tea." The idea of time has vanished now, as you were deeply engaged. In Samadhi, the past and present become one. There is simultaneous knowledge. Everything is present for the Yogi. Everything is here. Everything is now only.

The more you are concentrated, the more you are not aware of time. This is the test for deep concentration.

When the mind is fully occupied in the affairs of the war, the soldier does not feel any serious injury of a gun-shot wound in the leg. He is not aware of the loss of a large quantity of blood also. He has great concentration in war. He is not conscious of his body for the time being. When the excitement is over, when he sees some blood spots on his clothing, he comes to consciousness. Then only he is alarmed a bit. When the mind is intensely fond of anything, there will be no perception of pain even if destruction awaits the body. When the mind is completely drowned in any object, who else is there to observe and feel the actions of the body?

There are five Yoga Bhumikas or stages or five states of mind, viz., (1) Kshipta (wandering); (2) Mudha (forgetful); (3) Vikshipta (gathering mind); (4) Ekagrata (one-pointed); (5) Nirudha (controlled or well-restrained). In Kshipta state the rays of the mind are scattered. It is always wandering. In Mudha state, the man does not know anything. He is quite dull. He will harm others. In Vikshipta state, the mind is centered for a short time only; but wanders about for a long time. In Ekagrata state, it is one-pointed and concentrated. You can enter into Samadhi with the help of this mind. In Nirudha state, all the Vrittis are controlled. This is the state of Vritti-sunya. But Samskaras which are the seeds for Vrittis are here. No Yoga is possible in the first three states of mind. Yoga is possible in the fourth and fifth states only.

10. Benefits of Dharana

परमाणुपरममहत्त्वान्तोऽस्य वशीकारः । I-40

परमाणु finest atom, परममहत्त्व greatest infinity, अन्तः end, अस्य his (the man who concentrates), वशीकारः power.

His (one who concentrates) power extends from the finest atom to the greatest infinity.

NOTES

The mind can easily meditate by steady practice on the most minute as well as the biggest object. This is the proper test for concentration. He has mastery in concentration starting from the smallest of atoms to infinity. He has full concentration. He does not want any more practice.

He who practises concentration will possess a very good health and very cheerful mental vision. Through concentration you will get penetrative insight. Subtle esoteric meanings will flash out in the field of mental consciousness. You will understand the inner depths of philosophical significance when you read the Gita or the Upanishads with concentration. Those who practise concentration evolve quickly. They can do any work with greater efficiency. What others can do in six hours, can be done by one who does concentration, within half an hour. What others can read in six hours, can be read by one who does concentration, within half an hour. Concentration purifies and calms the surging emotions, strengthens the current of thought and clarifies the ideas. Concentration keeps a man in his material progress also. He will have a very good out-turn of work in his office. What was cloudy and hazy before, becomes clearer and definite; what was difficult before becomes easy now; and what was complex, bewildering and confusing before, comes easily within the mental grasp. You can achieve anything through concentration. Nothing is impossible for one who practises regular concentration.

11. Instructions on Dharana

1. Purify the mind first through the practice of Yama and Niyama. Then take to the practice of Dharana. Concentration without purity is of no use. There are some

occultists who have concentration. But they do not have good character. This is the reason why they do not make any progress in the spiritual path. Ethical perfection is of paramount importance.

2. A man whose mind is filled with passion and all sorts of fantastic desires can hardly concentrate on any object even for a second. His mind will be jumping like a monkey.

3. There can be no concentration without something upon which the mind may rest. The mind can be fixed easily on a pleasing object such as jasmine flower, mango or a loving friend. It is very difficult in the beginning to fix the mind on any object which it dislikes such as faecal matter, cobra, enemy, ugly face, etc.

4. Practise concentration till the mind is well-established on the object of concentration. When the mind runs away from the object of concentration bring it back again to the object.

5. It is very difficult to practise concentration when one is very hungry and when one is suffering from an acute disease.

6. Train the mind in concentrating on various objects gross and subtle and of various sizes big, medium and small. In course of time a strong habit of concentration will be formed. The moment you sit for concentration, the mood will come at once, quite easily.

7. For a neophyte the practice of concentration is disgusting and tiring. He has to cut new grooves in the mind and the brain. After some time, say two or three months' regular practice, he gets great interest. He enjoys a new kind of happiness. He becomes restless if he fails to enjoy this new kind of happiness one day. Concentration is the only way to get rid of worldly miseries and tribulations. You have taken this physical body only to achieve concentration and through concentration to realise the Self.

CHAPTER XI

SAMYAMA

1. What Is Samyama

त्रयमेकत्र संयमः । III-4

त्रयम् the three, एकत्र together, संयमः Samyama.

The three (Dharana, Dhyana and Samadhi) together constitute Samyama.

NOTES

Samyama means perfect control of the mind. Here it is a technical name for three inseparable processes of Dharana, Dhyana and Samadhi taken collectively. By the practice of Samyama, the Yogi gets knowledge and powers. The three processes are practised on any one object successively at the same time. The five Angas of Yoga are intended to purify the body, Prana and the senses. These three practices purify the mind. They constitute the very basis of Yoga. With the help of these three, the Yogi dives deep within and brings out the pearl of knowledge of anything. Samyama is the name given to the combined practice of Dharana, Dhyana and Samadhi at one and the same time. By Samyama on external objects he gets various Siddhis and hidden knowledge of the universe of Tanmatras, etc. By concentration on Indriyas, Ahamkara and mind, etc., he gets various powers and experiences. These things are explained in the subsequent Sutras.

2. Samyama As Antaranga Sadhana

त्रयमन्तरङ्गं पूर्वेभ्यः । III-7

त्रयम् the three, अन्तरङ्गम् more internal than, पूर्वेभ्यः the preceding.

(123)

The three (Dharana, Dhyana and Samadhi) are more
internal than the preceding (Yama, Niyama, Asana,
Pranayama and Pratyahara).

These three constitute the Yoga proper. The five
accessories are the external means of Yoga. These three
directly bring Samadhi. The other five purify the body,
Prana and Indriyas. Hence these three are called
Antaranga Sadhana.

3. Samyama As Bahiranga Sadhana

तदपि बहिरङ्गं निर्बीजस्य । III-8

तदपि even that (Samyama), बहिरङ्गम् external, निर्बीजस्य to
the seedless Samadhi.

Even that (Samyama) is external to the seedless Samadhi.

Nirbija Samadhi or Asamprajnata Samadhi is the final
goal of Raja Yoga. Compared to that, this Samyama
(Dharana, Dhyana, Samadhi) also is external or indirect. It
is also preparatory. Here there is Alambana or something
for the mind to depend upon; whereas in Nirbija Samadhi,
there is nothing for the mind to depend upon. It is
Niralambana. It is Nirbija (seedless) Samadhi.

4. Benefits of Samyama

तज्जयात् प्रज्ञालोकः । III-5

तज्जयात् by conquest of Samyama, प्रज्ञा-लोकः the light of
Prajna or the stage of cognition.

By the conquest of Samyama, comes the stage of cognition.

As Samyama becomes firmer and firmer, so does the
knowledge of Samadhi become more and more lucid. This
is the fruit of the practice of Samyama. Samyama should
become very natural. Then the knowledge flashes like

anything. Samyama is a powerful weapon for the Yogi. Just as the archer aims at the gross objects at first, and then takes to subtle objects, so also the Yogi does Samyama on gross objects and then takes to subtle objects. He does great deal of practice and ascends the Yogic ladder rung by rung.

5. Samyama on External Objects

(1) On the Sun

भुवनज्ञानं सूर्ये संयमात् । III-27

भुवन the worlds, ज्ञानम् knowledge, सूर्ये on the Sun, संयमात् by Samyama.

By Samyama on the Sun comes the knowledge of the worlds.

NOTES

Bhuvanas are Lokas or worlds. All Lokas are included in one Brahmanda. There are seven upper worlds and seven lower worlds as given below:

Higher Worlds	Lower Worlds
1. Bhu Loka	1. Sutala Loka
2. Bhuvar Loka	2. Vitala Loka
3. Swar Loka	3. Talatala Loka
4. Mahar Loka	4. Mahatala Loka
5. Jana Loka	5. Rasatala Loka
6. Tapo Loka	6. Atala Loka
7. Satya Loka	7. Patala Loka

(2) On the Moon

चन्द्रे ताराव्यूहज्ञानम् । III-28

चन्द्रे on the moon, तारा of the stars, व्यूह systems, ज्ञानम् knowledge.

By Samyama on the moon, comes the knowledge of the regions of stars.

(3) On the Pole Star

ध्रुवे तद्गतिज्ञानम् । III-29

ध्रुवे on the Pole star, तद्गति movements of the stars, ज्ञानम् knowledge.

By Samyama on the Pole Star, comes the knowledge of the movements of the stars.

(4) Samyama on Elephant

बलेषु हस्तिबलादीनि । III-25

बलेषु the strength, हस्ति elephant, बल strength, आदीनि and others.

By Samyama on the strength of elephants and others, comes their strength.

NOTES

By practising Samyama on Hanuman, the Yogi gets the power of Hanuman. By Samyama on Vayu, he gets the powers of Vayu. In this way by doing Samyama on any object, you will get its power.

(5) Samyama on the Form of Body

कायरूपसंयमात्तद्ग्राह्यशक्तिस्तम्भे चक्षुःप्रकाशासंयोगेऽन्तर्धानम् । III-21

कायरूप the form of the body, संयमात् by Samyama, तद्ग्राह्यशक्ति the power of comprehension, स्तम्भे being checked, चक्षुः eye, प्रकाश light, असंयोगे being severed, अन्तर्धानम् disappearance.

By Samyama on the form of the body, the power of comprehension being checked, and the connection between the eye and light being severed, comes the disappearance of the body.

NOTES

The body is made up of five Tattvas. On account of

colour, the body becomes an object of perception. When the Yogi does Samyama with reference to the form of the body, the operation of the perceptibility of colour which is responsible for perception of the body is checked. The Yogi severes the connection between the light of his body and the eye of the perceiver. Hence disappearance of his body follows. The same holds true of the other organs also. He can do Samyama on the sounds, touches, tastes and smells; their perceptibility being checked, there is no contact with the tympanum, skin, tongue, nose. Therefore, these disappear. Yogi has got the power of separating the form from the materials which go to constitute his body.

(6) Samyama on Sense-organs

एतेन शब्दाद्यन्तर्धानमुक्तम् । III-22

एतेन by this, शब्दाद्यन्तर्धानम् the making of words, etc., disappear, उक्तम् is explained.

By this the making of words, etc., disappear is explained.

NOTES

Refer to the previous Sutra. The Yogi does Samyama and disconnects the contact of the sounds, touches, tastes and smells from the tympanum, skin, tongue and nose respectively. Then disappearance of these take place.

(7) Samyama on the Signs

प्रत्ययस्य परचित्तज्ञानम् । III-19

प्रत्ययस्य on the signs of, परचित्त of other minds, ज्ञानम् knowledge.

By Samyama on the signs (of others), comes the knowledge of their minds.

NOTES

When the Yogi does Samyama on certain signs, such as the complexion, voice, or any such sign on the body of others, he understands the state or the nature of the mind

of others. Some astrologers give predictions correctly by
doing Samyama on the signs of his clients and by studying
their minds.

(8) Samyama on Mind

न च तत्सालम्बनं तस्याविषयीभूतत्वात् । III-20

न not, च and, तत् its (mind's), आलम्बनम् support or
contents, तस्य its, विषयी subject, भूतत्वात् beyond.

**(By Samyama on the signs) not the contents of the mind,
for the subject is beyond.**

NOTES

In the previous Sutra it is stated that one can have the
knowledge of the nature of mind by doing Samyama on the
signs. This Sutra states that one can know the nature of the
mind by that and not the contents of the mind, i.e., the
particular thought of mind. In order to know the contents
another man's mind, the Yogi performs a second Samyama
on the heart (III-35).

(9) Samyama on Time

क्षणतत्क्रमयोः संयमाद्विवेकजं ज्ञानम् । III-53

क्षण a small point of time, तत्क्रमयोः over their succession,
संयमात् by Samyama, विवेकजम् ज्ञानम् discriminative
knowledge.

**By Samyama on a small point of time comes the
discriminative knowledge.**

NOTES

Kshana is the smallest unit of time that cannot be
further divided. By doing Samyama on this smallest unit of
time and the order in which they follow one another comes
discrimination of everything which helps the Yogi to free
himself from the tempting invitation of Devas. Years,
months and days are made up of Kshana only. Kshana
constitutes time. There is slight interval between two

Kshanas. There is nothing which is not related to time. Therefore, by Samyama on Kshana, the Yogi surely gets knowledge of everything. Therefore he cannot be allured by the false representation of the Devas. Two moments cannot co-exist. The uninterrupted sequence of the first moment and of the one which follows, is what is called succession or order.

(10) Effect of Samyama on Time

जातिलक्षणदेशैरन्यताऽनवच्छेदात्तुल्ययोस्ततः प्रतिपत्तिः । III-54

जाति class, लक्षण characteristics, देश position, अन्यता separateness, अनवच्छेदात् not differentiated, तुल्ययोः similar things, ततः thereby, प्रतिपत्तिः the distinction.

The similar things are thereby (by Samyama) distinguished when not separately differentiated by class, characteristics and position.

NOTES

Things are generally differentiated by the class or species, peculiar characteristics and place. When all these three fail to differentiate the things, the discrimination that is described in the above Sutra will doubtless help the Yogi. "This is a horse. This is brown-coloured horse." This is the differentiation by Lakshana or signs. "That camel is in front. This elephant is behind." This is the differentiation by place. All such knowledge can be had by Samyama on time. Discrimination will bring the knowledge of Purusha. The ignorance which is the root cause for human sufferings and tribulations, which makes you identify yourself with the physical body will be destroyed thereby.

(11) Samyama on Ear and Ether

श्रोत्राकाशयोः संबन्धसंयमादिद्विव्यं श्रोत्रम् । III-42

श्रोत्राकाशयोः between ether and ear, सम्बन्ध relation, संयमात् by Samyama, दिव्यम् divine, श्रोत्रम् hearing.

By Samyama on the relation of the ear and ether, comes the divine hearing.

NOTES

The Yogi can hear any subtle sound from any distance through this Samyama, by simple willing. He acquires the full power of the organ of hearing. Similarly by connecting with the Adhistana-bhutas (Vayu, Tejas, Apas and Prithvi), he can acquire the full powers of other organs also.

(12) Samyama on Ether and Body

कायाकाशयोः सम्बन्धसंयमाल्लघुतूल-
समापत्तेश्चाकाशगमनम् । III-43

कायाकाशयोः between body and ether, सम्बन्ध relation, संयमात् by Samyama, लघु light, तूल cotton, समापत्ते attaining, च and, आकाश through ether, गमनम् passage.

By Samyama on the relation between ether and body, to the Yogi, attaining the lightness of cotton, comes the power of passage through ether (air).

NOTES

The body becomes very light by the practice of Samyama on the relation between ether and body or on the lightness of cotton. Hence the Yogi can move anywhere in the space like a bird. He can walk on the string of a spider's web. He can move along the rays of the sun.

Those who know Sammohana Vidya or Indrajala also can move in the air. But, this is Jala (trick) only. Not real. He remains in the ground only. If you take any photograph, you will not get picture of the man in the air. A Hatha Yogi who has Siddhi in Khechari Mudra can also fly in the air.

6. Samyama on Internal Centres

(1) On the Modifications of Mind

परिणामत्रयसंयमादतीतानागतज्ञानम् । III-16

परिणामत्रय the three modifications of mind, संयमात् by Samyama, अतीत past, अनागत future, ज्ञानम् knowledge.

By Samyama on the three modifications of mind, comes the knowledge of the past and future.

NOTES

The threefold changes are mentioned in Sutra III-13. When direct knowledge of the threefold changes is obtained by means of Samyama, knowledge of their past and future is obtained.

The Yogi plunges deep into the source, i.e., the Samskaras by Samyama, and gets the knowledge of the past and future. He can do it in the twinkling of an eye. When once you know the technique, you can acquire the knowledge through Samyama. This is given in Sutra III-18.

(2) Videha Can Pass Out of Body

बहिरकल्पिता वृत्तिर्महाविदेहा ततः प्रकाशावरणक्षयः । III-44

बहिरकल्पिता passing out of the body, वृत्तिः acting, महाविदेहा great Videha or bodiless, ततः by that, प्रकाश light, आवरण veil, क्षयः destruction.

The great Videha (bodiless) is passing out of the body and functioning there, and by that comes the destruction of the veil of light.

NOTES

By practising Samyama on the real modifications of the mind when it is separated from the body—the state known as the 'the great bodiless'—all coverings can be removed from the light of knowledge. In ordinary persons the mind is confined to this little body only. He identifies himself with this body only. In a Yogi this mind goes outside the body and feels all-pervading nature (omnipresence). The mind feels that it is independent of the physical body. This is called 'Maha-videha' or 'great bodiless'. The Yogi can do Parakaya Pravesa (entering another body) with this mind.

The Yogi can enter another body without the Samyama mentioned in Sutra III-39. In this state knowledge of any and every description is within his easy reach.

His mind is full of Sattva as the covering of light is destroyed. Rajas and Tamas constitute this covering.

This Sutra is the quintessence of the meditational technique described by Patanjali, by which we are introduced to the very heart of the matter so pithily and crisply. This Sutra makes out that there are two ways of the functioning of the mind, one in the form of a thought of an external object and another as a total and comprehensive operation in which the object in meditation becomes inseparable from its thought. Usually such an exercise is not humanly possible. Who can think in such a way that the object enters the mind itself and the object becomes the thought and the thought becomes the object! This is a staggering suggestion given by the Sutra that the entire world can enter into the process of thinking. If the universe enters the mind and the mind enters the universe, this exercise is said to lead to immediate liberation.

(3) Samyama on Samskaras

संस्कारसाक्षात्करणात्पूर्वजातिज्ञानम् । III-18

संस्कार impressions of mind, साक्षात्करणात् by direct perception, पूर्वजाति previous birth, ज्ञानम् knowledge.

By Samyama and direct perception of the Samskaras (impressions of mind), comes the knowledge of the previous births.

NOTES

All actions, enjoyments and experiences leave the impressions in the subconscious mind in the form of subtle impressions or residual potencies. The Samskaras are the roots for causing again Jati, life and experiences of pleasure and pain (vide Sutra II-13). Revival of Samskaras induce memory. The Yogi dives deep inside and comes in

direct contact with these Samskaras. He directly perceives
them through his inner Yogic vision. By Samyama on these
Samskaras, he acquires knowledge of previous lives.

Samskaras are of two kinds, those appearing as habits
and causing memories and afflictions; and those appearing
as virtue and vice and bringing fruits. The direct
knowledge of the Samskaras is not possible without the
knowledge of space, time and operative cause. The Yogi
gets help from Parinama, Chesta, Nirodha, Sakti, Jivana
and Dharma (mind-change, activity, suppression, ideation
in action, physical life and characteristics respectively). By
doing Samyama on the Samskaras of others he gets the
knowledge of their past lives also.

(4) Samyama on Indriyas

ग्रहणस्वरूपास्मितान्वयार्थवत्त्वसंयमादिन्द्रियजयः । III-48

ग्रहण the power of cognition, स्वरूप own essential
nature, अस्मित egoism, अन्वय qualities, अर्थवत्त्व
purposefulness, संयमात् by Samyama, इन्द्रियजयः mastery over
senses.

**By Samyama on the power of cognition, the essential own
nature, egoism, qualities and purposefulness or condition of
senses, comes the mastery over senses (organs).**

NOTES

Just as there are five conditions for the elements (*vide*
Sutra III-45), so also there are five states or conditions for
the organs. The power of cognition is the power which
every organ possesses such as seeing, smelling, hearing,
tasting and touching; their nature refers to the knowledge
which each brings from the object of cognition; egoism
refers to the individual consciousness that is present in all
the acts; qualities are Sattva, Rajas and Tamas;
purposefulness is Bhoga and Apavarga, enjoyment and
emancipation.

If the Indriyas remain quiet without moving towards

objects, and if they are fixed in their respective places, the Yogi enjoys a peculiar, indescribable Ananda. This is Sananda Samadhi.

(5) Siddhis for Samyama on Indriyas

ततो मनोजवित्वं विकरणभावः प्रधानजयश्च । III-49

ततो thence, मनोजवित्वं quick movement like the mind, विकरणभावः perception without the Indriyas (senses), प्रधानजयः mastery over Pradhana (nature), च and.

Thence comes to the body the power of quick movement like mind and perception without the Indriyas (senses) and mastery over nature.

NOTES

Madhu-patrika is the name given to the mastery over Bhutas, Indriyas and Pradhana (the combined Bhuta Jaya, Indriya Jaya and Pradhana Jaya). In this state the Yogi attains Ritambara Prajna. 'Tatah' means from the mastery of Indriyas. Mastery over the elements brings the eight Siddhis and Kaya Siddhi. Indriya Jaya brings Manojavitam, independent power of the organs and mastery over the first cause i.e., Pradhana Jaya. 'Madhu-patrika' means as sweet as honey. The body gets the power of quick movements as the mind and the Indriyas to grasp the movements of the body independently.

(6) Samyama on Udana Vayu

उदानजयाज्जलपङ्ककण्टकादिष्वसङ्ग उत्क्रान्तिश्च । III-40

उदान Udana Vayu, जयात् by mastery over, जल-पङ्क-कण्टक-आदिषु water, mud, thorns and others, असङ्ग without any contact, उत्क्रान्तिः ascension or can die at will, च and.

By acquiring mastery over Udana Vayu, the Yogi will not have any contact with water, mud, thorns and others, and can die at will.

NOTES

It is Udana Vayu that separates the astral body from the physical body at the time of death. By control over this current he becomes very, very light. In conjunction with Prana Vayu, Udana plays an important part in governing the motion of lungs. Udana helps the function of deglutition or swallowing of food stuffs also. Jalasthamba and Vayusthamba are also done by control over Udana. By Samyama on this, the Yogi is not at all affected by water, thorns, etc.

(7) Samyama on Samana Vayu

समानजयात्प्रज्वलनम् । III-41

समान Samana Vayu, जयात् by mastery, प्रज्वलनम् effulgence.

By mastery over Samana Vayu, comes effulgence.

NOTES

The body of the Yogi who has mastered the current Samana Vayu is effulgent. He can create fire out of his body. Sage Sarabhanga after having Darshan of Sri Rama, created fire out of his physical body, burnt his physical body in this Yogic fire and with the Divya body (luminous body) entered Brahmaloka *(vide* Aranya Kanda of the Ramayana). Light flashes out from the body of the Yogi who has mastery over this Samana Vayu.

7. Samyama on Virtues

मैत्र्यादिषु बलानि । III-24

मैत्र्यादिषु friendliness and other virtues, बलानि powers.

By Samyama on friendliness and other virtues comes the power (to transmit same to others.)

NOTES

By the word 'Adishu' (and others), the other virtues Karuna, Mudita, etc., are included. By Samyama on these virtues, the Yogi develops these qualities to a very high degree and gets the power to infuse these qualities in others also. Yogis radiate these qualities on all sides.

8. Samyama on Discrimination

सत्त्वपुरुषान्यताख्यातिमात्रस्य सर्वभावाधिष्ठातृत्वं
सर्वज्ञातृत्वं च । III-50

सत्त्व purity, पुरुष Púrusha, the Soul, अन्यताख्यातिमात्रस्य who recognises the distinctive relation between, सर्वभाव over all states, अधिष्ठातृत्वम् supremacy (omnipotence), सर्वज्ञातृत्वम् omniscience, च and.

By Samyama on the distinctive relation between Sattva (purity) and Purusha (the soul), come the powers of omnipotence and omniscience.

NOTES

The relation between Sattva and Purusha is also taken as the relation between Prakriti and Purusha. This Siddhi is called as Visoka which means 'without sorrow.' The Yogi who has these Siddhis will have no sorrow in any condition.

9. Samyama on Sabdha and Artha

शब्दार्थप्रत्ययानामितरेतराध्यासात्सङ्करस्तत्प्रविभाग संयमात्
सर्वभूतरुतज्ञानम् । III-17

शब्द word, अर्थ meaning, प्रत्ययानाम् knowledge of these, इतरेतर-अध्यासात्-सङ्करः are confused with one another and appear as one because of similarity, तत्-प्रविभाग their distinctions, संयमात् by Samyama, सर्वभूत of all living beings, रुतज्ञानम् knowledge of sounds.

By Samyama on the distinctions of the word, meaning and knowledge which are confused with one another and appear as one because of similarity, comes the knowledge of the sounds of all living beings.

NOTES

In ordinary persons word, meaning and knowledge are mixed up together. But, the Yogi can separate them. By making Samyama on any sound he can understand the meaning of any sound. Sphota is something indescribable (state of sound) which eternally exists apart from the letters forming any word, and is yet inseparably connected with it, for it reveals itself on the utterance of that word. It is subtle. 'Sphota' means 'bursting like a bubble'. Sphota is of two kinds, viz., Patha Sphota and Vakhya Sphota. Patha Sphota is that power which brings out the knowledge of a word as soon as it is uttered. Vakhya Sphota is that power which brings knowledge of a sentence as soon as it is uttered. The Udana Vayu connects itself with the chest and other seven places viz., larynx, root of the tongue, teeth, lips, palate, nose and head and cause the arising of all letters. The Yogi can understand the meaning of the sounds uttered by animals, the language of animals and birds, the music of nature and the internal Anahata sounds.

10. Samyama on Karma

सोपक्रमं निरुपक्रमं च कर्म

तत्संयमादपरान्तज्ञानमरिष्टेभ्यो वा । III-23

सोपक्रमं quick in fructification, निरुपक्रमं slow in fructification, च and, कर्म works, तत्-संयमात् Samyama over these, अपरान्त of death, ज्ञानम् knowledge, अरिष्टेभ्यः by portents, वा or.

Karmas (works) are of two kinds, viz., those that are to be fructified quickly and those that will bring fruits slowly (at a later date). By Samyama over these or by portents, the Yogi gets the knowledge of (the time of) his death.

NOTES

A wet cloth, when well squeezed, dries up quickly. Similarly some Karmas bring fruits quickly. A wet cloth full of water dries up slowly. Similarly some Karmas bring fruits slowly. A Yogi by his Yogic power takes several

bodies and exhausts all the Karmas that bring fruits slowly.
Pattinattu Swami, a well-known Jnani, exhausted the
influences of Saturn planet that would last for 7½ years in
7½ Naligas (3 hours). Portents (Arishta) are certain
occurrences that cause fear.

They are of three kinds, viz., Adhyatmika,
Adhibhautika and Adhidaivika. The Yogi will find out the
exact date, hour and minute of his death by Samyama over
the Karmas. Yoga is an exact science. In fact it is the
Science of sciences. By the knowledge of the portents also,
the Yogi can find out the date of his death.

11. Samyama on Chakras and Nadis

(1) On Nabhi Chakra

नाभिचक्रे कायव्यूहज्ञानम् । III-30

नाभिचक्रे on the Plexus of Navel, कायव्यूह the arrangement
of the body, ज्ञानम् knowledge.

**By Samyama on the Chakra (plexus) of navel, comes the
knowledge of the body.**

NOTES

Nabhi Chakra is known as Manipura Chakra according
to Tantra Sastra. By practising Samyama on this Chakra,
the Yogi gets the knowledge of the construction of the
body, the seven Dhatus, etc. The description of different
Chakras, their presiding deities, the number of petals in
each, the functions of each Chakra are all given in my book
'Kundalini Yoga'.

(2) On the Visuddha Chakra

कण्ठकूपे क्षुत्पिपासानिवृत्तिः । III-31

कण्ठकूपे the pit of the throat, क्षुत्पिपासा hunger and thirst,
निवृत्तिः removal.

**By Samyama on (the Chakra at) the pit of the throat,
comes the removal of hunger and thirst.**

NOTES

At the pit of the throat, there is Visuddha Chakra. By Samyama on this Chakra, the Yogi becomes free from the afflictions of hunger and thirst.

(3) On Sahasrara Chakra

मूर्धज्योतिषि सिद्धदर्शनम् । III-33

मूर्धज्योतिषि on the light of the head, सिद्धदर्शनम् the Darshan (vision) of Siddhas (perfected Yogis).

By Samyama on the light of the head, comes the Darshan of Siddhas.

NOTES

Siddhas are those who move in space between earth and sky. Murdha is the crown of the head. Brahmarandhra or hole of Brahma is here. Coronal artery is connected with the Brahmarandhra. Just as the light leaks out through a hole in the door or window of a house, so also the light of Sattva leaks out through this hole of Brahma. Nirguna Upasakas select this place for their abstract meditation. This centre at the head is Sahasrara Chakra. Samyama at this Chakra will bring divine visions.

(4) On Anahata Chakra

हृदये चित्तसंवित् । III-35

हृदये at the heart, चित्तसंवित् knowledge of the mind.

By Samyama on the heart, comes the knowledge of (the contents of) the mind.

NOTES

At the heart the centre is Anahata Chakra. This is a very important centre for meditation.

(5) On Kurma Nadi

कूर्मनाड्याम् स्थैर्यम् । III-32

कूर्मनाड्याम् on the Kurma Nadi, स्थैर्यम् steadiness (of body).

By Samyama on the Kurma Nadi (the tube within the chest), comes the steadiness of the body.

NOTES

Kurma is one of the five sub-Pranas. It shuts and opens the eyelids. The astral tube by which this sub-Prana passes is Kurma Nadi. This Nadi is in the chest below the throat. By Samyama on this Nadi, the Yogi gets steadiness of the body.

(6) On the Inner Light

प्रवृत्त्यालोकन्यासात्सूक्ष्मव्यवहितविप्रकृष्टज्ञानम् । III-26

प्रवृत्त्यालोक the inner light (of the lotus within the heart), न्यासात् by contemplation or by practising Samyama, सूक्ष्म subtle, व्यवहित obscured, veiled, विप्रकृष्ट remote, ज्ञानम् knowledge.

By Samyama on the inner light (of the lotus within the heart), comes the knowledge of the subtle, the obscured and the remote.

NOTES

The inner light referred to here is already explained in Sutra I-36. The Yogi develops clairvoyance. He can see vividly hidden treasures. A Yogi who lives in a Himalayan cave can clearly see things in the United States of America. He can see the invisible electrons and atoms. He can read what is written in a sealed envelope.

(7) On One's Own Self

सत्त्वपुरुषयोरत्यन्तासंकीर्णयोः प्रत्ययाविशेषो भोगः परार्थत्वात्
स्वार्थसंयमात् पुरुषज्ञानम् । III-36

सत्त्व purity, पुरुषयोः of the Purusha, अत्यन्तासंकीर्णयोः absolutely distinct from each other, प्रत्यय distinction,

अविशेषः absence, भोगः experience, परार्थत्वात् for the sake of another, स्वार्थ on himself, संयमात् by Samyama, पुरुषज्ञानम् the knowledge of Purusha.

Experience comes from the absence of discrimination between Sattva and Purusha that are absolutely distinct from each other. This (enjoyment) being for another (Purusha), knowledge of Purusha comes by Samyama on himself.

NOTES

Purusha only can know Himself as He is Self-luminous. Buddhi, in the presence of Chaitanya Purusha, shines as intelligent through the Chaitanya of Purusha. Purusha is reflected in clear Sattva (Buddhi) and therefore he has energised and magnetised the Buddhi. Buddhi foolishly imagines that all experiences are its own acts. This confused identification of the two is the cause for experiences and enjoyment. The action of Sattva or Buddhi is for another (Purusha) and not for himself.

(8) Benefits of Samyama on One's Self

ततः प्रतिभश्रावणवेदनादर्शास्वादवार्ता जायन्ते । III-37

ततः from that (Samyama), प्रतिभः intuition, श्रावण clairaudience, वेदन higher touch, आदर्श clairvoyance, आस्वाद higher taste, वार्ता higher smell, जायन्ते arises, proceed.

From that (Samyama) arises the knowledge of clairaudience, higher touch, clairvoyance, higher taste and higher smell through intuition.

NOTES

The five kinds of knowledge derived from the functioning of the five Jnana Indriyas are now derived by the power of Pratibha without any Samyama (*vide* Sutra III-34). The Yogi gets the power of Sravana, the capacity to hear remote sounds; Vedana, the capacity to touch remote objects; Adarsha, the capacity to see remote objects; Asvada, the capacity to taste remote objects; and Varta, the capacity to sense the smell of remote objects, and other Siddhis through intuition. The fruits of Pratibha is explained in the Sutra III-34.

12. Fruits of Pratibha

प्रातिभाद्वा सर्वम् । III-34

प्रातिभाद् by intuition, वा or, सर्वम् all (knowledge).

By the power of intuition, comes the knowledge of all knowledge.

NOTES

If a Yogi has the power of Pratibha he gets all Siddhis and knowledge without practising Samyama at all. Pratibha is called Taraka Jnana, the knowledge that leads to Moksha or emancipation. Pratibha is prescience or intuition. When the mind becomes very, very pure and is filled with Sattva, spontaneous illumination dawns. The Taraka Jnana is explained in Sutra III-55.

13. What Is Taraka

तारकं सर्वविषयं सर्वथाविषयमक्रमं चेति विवेकजं ज्ञानम् । III-55

तारकम् intuition or the knowledge that gives liberation, सर्वविषयम् relating to all objects, सर्वथाविषयम् in all conditions, अक्रमम् having no succession or simultaneous, च and, इति this, विवेकजं ज्ञानम् discriminative knowledge.

The knowledge born of discrimination is Taraka, relating to all objects in every condition and without having any succession.

NOTES

In Sutra III-34, a description is given of Taraka Jnana. The discriminative knowledge described in Sutra III-53 results into Taraka. It relates to all objects from Pradhana down to Bhutas and also all conditions of these objects. Further this knowledge is simultaneous. Everything is

'present' only. Past and future are blended in the present.
Everything is 'now' only. There is no succession or order.
The Yogi becomes a 'Sarvajna' and 'Sarva-vit' —
all-knowing and all-understanding. Madhubhumi is a part
of this Taraka Jnana only. Pratibha consists in the capacity
to comprehend things which are hidden or veiled, remote
or past or future or extremely subtle. The whole
knowledge is revealed to the Yogi who has Pratibha.

14. Parakaya Pravesa

(1) Mind Enters Another Body

बन्धकारणशैथिल्यात् प्रचारसंवेदनाच्च
चित्तस्य परशरीरावेशः । III-39

बन्ध bondage, कारण cause, शैथिल्यात् on relaxation, प्रचार
the method of passages, संवेदनात् by the knowledge, च and,
चित्तस्य of the mind, परशरीर other's body, आवेशः entering
into.

**The mind (of a Yogi) enters another body, by relaxation of
the cause of bondage and by the knowledge of the method of
passing.**

NOTES

On account of Karmas the mind is bound to a
particular body. By the force of Samadhi, the Karmas
which chain the mind to a body become loosened. By the
destruction of the bonds imposed by Karma, and by
knowing the passages through which he can re-enter his
own body, the Yogi withdraws his mind from his body and
enters another body. When the mind enters another body,
the organs also follow the Indriyas, just as the common
bees follow the queen bee. The knowledge of the passage
for the mind helps the Yogi in entering another body and
re-entering his own body. Sri Sankaracharya entered the
dead body of the Rajah of Banaras and his disciple
Padmapada took care of his physical body. Vikramaditya

also knew this Yogic process. He entered the body of others. A Rishi entered the body of a dead cowherd to look after the cows and had a new name Tirumular, the reputed author of Tirumantram in Tamil. Hastamalaka, disciple of Sri Sankaracharya, had another body previously. He entered the body of a small boy and remained silent on the banks of a river. Sri Sankara took him and made him as his disciple. A Yogi can enter the body of a living man and operate through his body and mind. Mind is Vibhu or all-pervading. Cosmic mind is Hiranyagarbha. When the individual mind is purified, it becomes one with the cosmic mind.

(2) Source of Created Minds

निर्माणचित्तान्यस्मितामात्रात् । IV-4

निर्माणचित्तानि created minds, अस्मितामात्रात् from egoism alone.

Created minds emanate from egoism alone.

NOTES

The Yogi wants to exhaust all Karmas quickly. Therefore he multiplies himself and takes many bodies. He manufactures minds for these bodies out of Ahamkara, egoism. He may like to enjoy several things at the same time. For this simultaneous enjoyment he creates several bodies and several minds through his Yogic powers. The Yogi has full command over Mahat Tattva. Egoism proceeds from Mahat Tattva. So there is no difficulty for a Yogi to create many minds as he likes. He taps the source for all minds, and manufactures several minds from the great reservoir over which he has absolute control. These minds are called 'Nirmana Chittani—created minds.' These new manufactured bodies are called 'Kaya-vyuha'. The Yogi keeps with him the control for these bodies.

(3) Original Mind Is the Director

प्रवृत्तिभेदे प्रयोजकं चित्तमेकमनेकेषाम् । IV-5

प्रवृत्तिभेदे difference in various functions, प्रयोजकम्
director, चित्तम् mind, एकम् one, अनेकेषाम् of the many
(minds).

**Though there is difference in various functions, the one
mind (Yogi's original mind) is the director of the many
(created minds).**

NOTES

The identity of one and the same individual is
preserved in all these manufactured bodies (Nirmana-
kayas) and minds (Nirmana-chittas). The Yogi draws in all
the created bodies and minds into himself as the sun draws
in his rays.

(4) The Play of Prakriti

जात्यन्तरपरिणामः प्रकृत्यापूरात् । IV-2

जात्यन्तर-परिणामः the transformation into another class
(species), प्रकृति of the nature, अपूरात् flow or filling up.

**The transformation into another class (species) is by the
flow of Prakriti (nature).**

NOTES

One body is changed into another of a different kind in
the same existence by the flow of Prakriti. The process of
changing the body is explained in the next Sutra.

(5) Causes in the Action of Prakriti

निमित्तमप्रयोजकं प्रकृतीनां वरणभेदस्तु ततः क्षेत्रिकवत् । IV-3

निमित्तम् incidental cause, अप्रयोजकम् those that do not
move into action, प्रकृतीनाम् creative causes, वरण obstacles,
भेदः pierce or remove, तु but, ततः from that, क्षेत्रिकवत् like a
husbandman (in a field).

**The incidental causes do not move the Prakriti into action,
but they remove the obstacles like a husbandman (in the
field).**

The husbandman removes the obstacles in the way of the water and the water then passes of itself from one field or bed to another field or bed. Even so, the virtuous deeds remove the obstacles that stand in the way of evolution of Prakriti (that stand in the way of getting another different body in the same existence). It is not the virtue that becomes the cause of the creative causes moving into action. Virtue becomes the cause of the removal of the vice, because they are diametrically opposed to each other.

Animal is hidden in vegetables; vegetable is hidden in minerals; man is hidden in animals; and God is hidden in man. When the obstacles are removed rapid evolution takes place.

Nature rushes in to work out the creative processes or evolution. Divinity is the very birth-right or heritage of man. When the obstacles are removed he becomes Purusha or Brahman or God. Ignorance and its effects, egoism, Raga, Dvesha, etc., act as barriers. Removal of these barriers allows the flow of knowledge, power and peace. All Yogic practices are best calculated to remove the barriers that stand in the way of the shutters of ignorance and egoism. The river of Jnana will flow by itself.

15. Samyama on Forms

स्थूलस्वरूपसूक्ष्मान्वयार्थवत्त्वसंयमाद्भूतजयः । III-45

स्थूल gross form, स्वरूप constant nature, सूक्ष्म subtle form, अन्वय qualities, अर्थवत्त्व purposefulness, संयमात् by Samyama, भूतजयः mastery over elements.

By Samyama on the gross form, substantive nature, subtle form, qualities and purposefulness of the elements, comes mastery over the elements.

NOTES

The gross form is that which is seen by the naked eyes.

Sabdha, Sparsa, Rupa, Rasa, Gandha are the Svarupa of
the five elements. The Tanmatras are subtle forms.
Qualities in them are the five general appearances,
conditions or states for the fire, motion for air,
all-pervading nature for the ether — these are the five
unchanging, real essential nature (Yathartha Svarupa) of
the five elements respectively. Anvaya means that which is
interpenetrating in all objects i.e., the three Gunas. That
Yogi who has mastery over the elements can command
nature. He can create anything by taking up materials from
the ocean of ether or Tanmatras. He can arrange and
rearrange the atoms of his body. He can create as many
bodies as he likes and work in all the bodies. Sri Jnana
Deva had this Siddhi. He made the Musjid and the walls of
his house to move. His sister, Mukta Bhai, prepared bread
out of the fire that emanated from his back. Visvamitra
also had this power. He created a third world for Trisanku.
You can also have this power if you practise this special
Samyama and understand the technique.

16. Eight Siddhis

ततोऽणिमादिप्रादुर्भावः कायसम्पत्तद्धर्मानभिघातश्च । III-46

ततः from that, अणिमादि the powers of Anima and others,
प्रादुर्भावः attainment of, कायसंपत् perfection of body, तत् their,
धर्म functions, अनभिघातः non-obstruction, च and.

**From that comes the attainment of the (eight major)
Siddhis, Anima, etc., and the perfection of body, and
non-obstruction of their functions.**

NOTES

It is stated that the Yogi attains the eight Siddhis and
perfection of body by the practice of the Samyama
explained in the previous Sutra. Here I will give a short
description of the eight Siddhis and in the next Sutra the
perfection of body is given.

The eight Siddhis are:

(1) **Anima**: The power to make oneself as minute as an atom. (2) **Mahima**: The power to expand oneself into space, (becoming big as huge as a mountain). (3) **Laghima**: The power to become as light as cotton. (4) **Garima**: The power to become as heavy as iron hill. (5) **Prapti**: The power of reaching anywhere (power to approach distant things), even to the moon, to touch it with tip of finger. (6) **Prakamya**: The power of having all desires realised. (7) **Ishatva**: The power to create. (8) **Vasitva**: The power to command all or the perfect control over elements.

Although a Yogi possesses all powers, he will never interfere with the smooth running of the world. He will not set the objects of the world topsy-turvy.

The Dharmas of the elements do not obstruct him. The earth does not interfere by cohesion with the action of a Yogi's body. He can even pass within the water for months together. The late Trailinga Swami of Banaras used to live for six months underneath the Ganga. The fire cannot burn him. The air cannot affect him. He can stand in Akasa.

17. Perfection of Body

रूपलावण्यबलवज्रसंहननत्वानि कायसम्पत् । III-47

रूप beauty, लावण्य gracefulness, बल strength, वज्रसंहननत्वानि adamantine hardness, कायसम्पत् perfection of body.

The perfection of body is (when it has) beauty, gracefulness, strength and adamantine hardness.

NOTES

The power to bear extreme heat and cold, the power to live without food and water (drawing the energy from his pure, strong, irresistible will), also come under the category 'Kaya-sampat.' As food is only a mass of energy, the body can be kept healthy and strong, if you can supply the body the energy from any other source such as sun, cosmic Prana, will, etc. Yogis know how to absorb the energy and utilise it for the economy of nature in the preservation of the body. Vayubakshana (eating or taking in air) is another way of maintaining the body. If the breath is stopped through Khechari Mudra, the Yogi can live by drinking the nectar that flows from Sahasrara Chakra.

Perfection of the body will come by the practice of Yoga systematically and by doing the Samyama described in Sutra III-45.

18. Other Means for Siddhis

जन्मौषधिमन्त्रतपः समाधिजाः सिद्धयः । IV-1

जन्म birth, औषधि drug, मन्त्र Mantras (incantation), तपः Tapas (austerities), समाधि superconscious state or trance, जाः born, सिद्धयः Siddhis (psychic powers).

The Siddhis are obtained by birth, drugs, Mantras, Tapas or by Samadhi.

NOTES

Devas get several Siddhis by birth. Kapila Muni was a born Siddha. Ashtavakra and Vama Deva spoke when they were dwelling in their mothers' wombs. Mandavya Muni who resided in Vindhya mountains acquired Siddhis by drugs and herbs called Rasayanas. The Yogis make Rasayanas and Siddha-kalpas and attain Kaya Siddhi by taking these preparations. They make Kalpas from sulphur, mercury, Nux-Vomica seeds, and Neem (Margosa) leaves, which possess wonderful powers.

By taking these Kalpas they can live as long as they like. There are certain herbs which stop hunger and thirst. In ancient days certain herbs had the power to talk with persons. Agasthya Muni gave curse to these herbs and then they ceased talking. One can get Siddhis by repetition of Mantras. Visvamitra attained Siddhis by repetition of Mantras. For getting Siddhis, one must have Sraddha.

Tapas is mortification of the body. Tapasvins do Kaya-klesa. Practice of Hatha Yogic Kriyas like Khechari

Mudra, etc., can give Siddhis. These come under the category of Tapas.

Yogis keep some mercury pills in their mouths and fly in the air. They prepare some ointment out of some herbs and apply it to their feet and move in the air. The Rasayanas can immortalise this physical body. They keep the physical body healthy and stronger in order to achieve the goal in this very life. Panchagni Tapas (sitting amidst five fires), standing on one leg with hands raised, living on Neem leaves, Krichara and Chandrayana Vrata are all forms of Tapas. They bring Siddhis. Standing in hot sun in summer, and in cold water in winter, living naked in ice are also a kind of Tapas. I met a Sadhu in Nimsar in 1932. He was standing on one leg from morning six o'clock till evening six o'clock. He had the help of a swing to lean upon occasionally.

19. Instruction on Samyama

(1) Gradual Practice

तस्य भूमिषु विनियोगः । III-6

तस्य its (Samyama's), भूमिषु by places or stages, विनियोगः application or practice.

Its (Samyama's) practice is by stages.

NOTES

It is difficult or impossible to ascend higher planes without mastering the lower planes. The Yogi knows the next stage himself. By conquest of one plane, he gets entry in the next stage. He who is carried away by the Siddhis cannot enjoy the happiness of Yoga. The image may be meditated with all parts; then without decorations or ornaments; then without limbs; then without any special identity; and lastly Abheda Dhyana, as not apart from the meditator or the 'Self.' The stages are those mentioned in Sutras II-27, I-17. No one who starts for Calcutta from Dehra Dun, reaches Calcutta without passing the intermediate stations. So is the case with Yoga also. One should practice Yoga stage by stage, step by step.

(2) Siddhis Are Obstacles

ते समाधावुपसर्गा व्युत्थाने सिद्धयः । III-38

ते they (Siddhis), समाधावुपसर्गाः obstacles in attaining Samadhi, व्युत्थाने to the out-going (mind), सिद्धयः Siddhis.

These Siddhis are obstacles in attaining Samadhi; but they are for the out-going mind.

NOTES

Samadhi here means Asamprajnata Samadhi. The Siddhis of Pratibha, etc., are obstacles. He who wants Kaivalya should ruthlessly shun or reject all Siddhis, as absolutely useless. He may get higher Siddhis, but he cannot become a Kritakritya. These come in the way of meditation as by-products. They should be ignored.

(3) Give Up Siddhis

तद्वैराग्यादपि दोषबीजक्षये कैवल्यम् । III-51

तद् for that (Siddhis), वैराग्यात् by dispassion, अपि even, दोषबीज the seed of bondage, क्षये destruction, कैवल्यम् independence.

By giving up even these (Siddhis) comes the destruction of the seed of bondage which brings Kaivalya or (independence).

NOTES

That Yogi, who rejects omnipotence and other Siddhis as mere straw, can attain the highest state of Kaivalya. All the causes of bondage beginning with Avidya mentioned in Sutra II-3 are destroyed when the Yogi rejects ruthlessly even these higher Siddhis. What are these Siddhis, when compared with the state of Kaivalya? Siddhis are in Maya or Prakriti. They are unreal and non-eternal. They are playful things only. Bija are the Purva-karma-samskaras

(Avidya). Kaivalya is also called 'Amanaska state' i. e., mindless condition. This Siddhi is called 'Samskara-sesha.'

(4) Avoid Temptations

स्थान्युपनिमन्त्रणे सङ्गस्मयाकरणं पुनरनिष्टप्रसङ्गात् । III-52

स्थान्युपनिमन्त्रणे when celestial beings invite, सङ्ग attachment, स्मय smile or happiness, अकरणम् not doing, पुनः again, अनिष्ट undesirable, प्रसङ्गात् possibility of contact.

The Yogi should give up attachment and smile or happiness when the celestial beings invite, as there is again the possibility of contact with undesirables.

NOTES

There are four classes of Yogins. (1) *Prathama-kalpika:* He is just a beginner or neophyte. The light is just appearing. He is just practising. He has not attained any Siddhis. This Yogi is just practising 'Savitarka Samadhi'. (2) *Madhu-bhumika:* One who has entered 'Nirvitarka Samadhi' and who has attained 'Ritambara Prajna.' This stage is also called Madhu-mati, because it brings the knowledge that gives satisfaction, just as honey does. (3) *Prajna Jyotis:* The Yogi has attained mastery over elements and senses. He has attained the stage of Madhu-pratika. (4) *Atikrantabhavaniya:* This Yogi has attained the Bhumikas of Visoka and Samskara-sesha. He has attained Kaivalya. Vyasa describes: 'His sole object is to make the mind latent in the Pradhana.'

The dangers mentioned in this Sutra will affect the Yogi who has entered the second stage. Devatas place various sorts of temptations before him. Many kinds of desires will try to overpower him. The Yogi will become proud and haughty, as he thinks that even Devatas have come to invite him. A downfall is sure to come. He will lose the zeal and earnestness in Yogic practice. False satisfaction will creep in. He will give up all Sadhana. This Sutra gives caution for the Yogi. You are fully aware of the story of Visvamitra, how he was allured by the celestial lady sent by Indra. The Devatas are full of jealousy. They do not like anyone to become a perfect Yogi. They put all sorts of obstacles. They come and invite the Yogi with sweet, cunning words and smile.

"Ride on this Vimana which will move in the Akasa. There are Kalpa Vriksha, Chintamani and Kamadhenu. There are beautiful, obedient nymphs. They will serve you nicely. Here are clairvoyance and clairaudience and a body of adamantine strength by drinking the nectar. You will not get old age and death." The Yogi, who is careful, who does not care a bit for these invitations and who has shunned all Siddhis can march direct to the goal and enjoy the Kaivalya or perfect Independence.

CHAPTER XII

DHYANA

1. What Is Dhyana

तत्र प्रत्ययैकतानता ध्यानम् । III-2

तत्र there, प्रत्यय mental effort or flow of perception, एकतानता continuous, ध्यानम् meditation.

A continuous flow of perception (or thought) is Dhyana (meditation).

NOTES

There is a continuous current in the mind of one object like the flow of water in a river (Pravaha). There is only one Vritti in the mind. It is Ekarupa-Vritti Pravaha. The meditation should be done at the appointed time daily. Then the meditative mood will come by itself without any effort. Sit also in the same place daily for meditation. Meditation on God must become habitual. First meditate on Lord Vishnu with all sorts of ornaments. Then meditate on Him without any ornament.

In the Isvara Gita you will find: "Concentration lasts as long as 12 Pranayamas; Dhyana lasts as long as 12 concentrations; and Samadhi lasts as long as 12 such Dhyanas."

Various objects of contemplation and meditation are given in the Chapters Dharana and Samyama. And so, repetition is avoided here. Major portion of the exercises and definitions given in the Chapters Dharana, Samyama and Samadhi, belong to this Chapter on 'Dhyana.' As I expressed previously, these Dharana, Dhyana and Samadhi cannot be separated. They form, as it were, one subject. The beginning portion of Dhyana is Dharana and the advanced portion is Samadhi. Since I have dealt with

(154)

Dharana, Samyama and Samadhi in detail, now I will close this Chapter with a few more instructions on Dhyana.

2. Instructions on Dhyana

1. Meditation is doubtless difficult. It will be very difficult, nay indeed impossible for a beginner to take to subtle meditation all at once. There must be graduated practices and the mind must be rendered very subtle for higher practices of concentration and meditation. Just as the archer first aims at gross things, target, etc., and then takes to subtle points, so also the student of Yoga should do gross concentration to start with and then take to subtle concentration practices. There must be a gradual ascent in the successive stages of Yoga. But, Yoga Brashtas like Jnana Deva, Sadasiva Brahman, Trailinga Swami and others can at once take to higher stages. Such persons are very, very rare indeed.

2. The object of meditation in the beginning must be Personal God, the body of Virat, or the four-armed Maha Vishnu, or the flute-bearer Lord Krishna or Rama or any other object. Later on, meditation can be practised on Impersonal God. In Savitarka meditation you will have a comprehensive understanding and knowledge of the objects, their excellences and defects, all the features, present, past and future, and also those near and remote, even those unheard of or unthought of. The whole knowledge of the objects and elements will be revealed to you. The name Samapatti is given to the four experiences collectively, Savitarka, Savichara, Sananda and Asmita. Sasmita Samadhi culminates in Dharmamegha Samadhi. Then comes absolute dispassion for him. This brings him Asamprajnata Samadhi.

3. Why do you read many books? It is of no use. The great book is within your heart. Open the pages of this inexhaustible book, the Source for all knowledge. You will know everything. What is that knowledge of Brahman or

the Source or Self? Close your eyes. Withdraw the senses. Merge deep in the Supreme Soul, the Light of lights, the Sun of suns. Complete knowledge will be revealed to you. You will have direct intuitional knowledge and divine wisdom by direct perception. All doubts will vanish now. All mental torments will disappear. All hot discussions, heated debates will terminate now. Peace and Jnana alone will remain.

4. Forget the body. Forget the surroundings. Forget friends and relatives. Forgetting these is the highest Sadhana. It helps meditation a great deal. By remembering God you can forget all these things. Merge within by practising deep, silent meditation. Taste the spiritual consciousness by withdrawing the mind from the sensual objects and fixing it on the object of meditation. This will lead you to Samadhi, the highest goal of Yogis.

5. You will have to note carefully whether you remain stationary in the spiritual path even after many years of meditation or whether you are progressing. Sometimes you may even retrograde or fall downwards also if you are not vigilant and careful, if your Vairagya wanes and if you are slack in meditation. Reaction may set in. Some practise meditation for a period of 15 years and yet they have not made any spiritual progress. Why? This is due to the lack of earnestness, Vairagya, keen longing for liberation and intense constant Sadhana. Just as water leaks out into the rat holes in the agricultural fields, so also energy is wasted in wrong channels through Raga and undercurrents, lurking, subtle desires. Suppressed desires also will manifest and harass you. Unconsciously you will become a victim to those desires.

6. When you advance in the spiritual practice, it will be very difficult for you to do both meditation and office work at the same time daily because the mind will undergo a double strain. It works in different grooves and channels with different Samskaras during Dhyana. It finds it difficult

to adjust itself to different kinds of uncongenial activity, as soon as it comes down from a higher plane of sublime thinking. The mind has to move in diametrically opposite direction. It gropes in the darkness. It gets bewildered, confused and puzzled. You might have noticed how the mind gets puzzled even in ordinary daily affairs of life when you go to a new place in matters of food, bath, rest and answering the calls of nature.

7. When you again sit for meditation in the evening you will have to struggle hard to wipe out the new worldly Samskāras you have gathered during the course of the day, and to get a calm, one-pointed mind again. This struggle, sometimes, brings on headache. The Prana which moves inwards in different grooves and channels and which is subtle during meditation has to move now in new different channels during worldly activities. It becomes very gross during work. During meditation the Prana is taken up to the head.

8. It would seem, therefore, that advanced Grihastha Yogic students will have to stop all worldly activities for some time as they advance in meditation, if they desire to advance further. They themselves will be forced to give up all works if they are really sincere. Work is a hindrance in meditation for advanced Yogic students. That is the reason why Lord Krishna says in the Gita: "For a sage who is seeking Yoga, action is called the means, for the same sage when he is enthroned in Yoga serenity is called the means." Then work and meditation become incompatibles like acid and alkalis or fire and water or light and darkness.

CHAPTER XIII

SAMADHI

1. What Is Samadhi

तदेवार्थमात्रानिर्भासं स्वरूपशून्यमिव समाधिः । III-3

तदेव the same (Dhyana), अर्थमात्र object alone, निर्भासम् shining, स्वरूप of its own form, शून्यम् devoid of, इव as it were, समाधिः Samadhi (superconscious state).

The same Dhyana is Samadhi when it shines with the object alone, as it were, devoid of itself.

NOTES

The thinker and the thought, the meditator and the meditated become one. The mind assumes or becomes the Dhyeya-rupa. The separate notions 'contemplation' and 'contemplated' and the 'contemplator' vanish. In the state of Samadhi the aspirant is not conscious of any external or internal objects. Just as the arrow-maker, having his mind engrossed in the arrow, knew not the king passing by his side, so also, the Yogi knows not anything when he is deep in his meditation.

2. Means for Samadhi

(1) One-pointed Mind

सर्वार्थतैकाग्रतयोः क्षयोदयौ चित्तस्य समाधिपरिणामः । III-11

सर्वार्थता all-pointedness (distractions), एकाग्रता one-pointedness (concentration), क्षय destructions (of the former), उदय appearance (of the latter), चित्तस्य or the mind, समाधिपरिणामः the modification of Samadhi.

The modification of Samadhi is the destruction of

(158)

all-pointedness (of mind) and appearance of one-pointedness
of mind (concentration of mind).

NOTES

With the destruction of the nature of the mind to run
after all objects and with the increase of the one-pointed
nature of the mind, the mind assumes the state of Samadhi.

(2) By Faith, Energy, etc.

श्रद्धावीर्यस्मृतिसमाधिप्रज्ञापूर्वक इतरेषाम् । I-20

श्रद्धा faith, वीर्य energy, स्मृति memory, समाधि Samadhi, प्रज्ञा
discernment, पूर्वक preceded by, इतरेषाम् for others.

**For others, it (Samadhi) is preceded by faith, energy,
memory and discernment.**

NOTES

In the previous Sutra the Samadhi for Prakriti-layas
and Videhas are given. In this Sutra Samadhi is given for
other Yogis.

Faith is the firm conviction of the mind as regards the
efficiency of the Yoga and the goal to be reached. Sincere
faith forces a man to do energetic action to realise the
fruit. This brings memory of all knowledge of the subject.
Then he concentrates and meditates. He then acquires
discrimination between the real and the unreal, and the
highest knowledge. Those who apply themselves diligently
to Yoga with perfect faith get themselves established in the
highest Asamprajnta Samadhi through Samprajnata which
brings in Para Vairagya. Faith sustains the Yogi like a kind,
affectionate mother.

(3) By Vairagya

तीव्रसंवेगानामासन्नः । I-21

तीव्र keen, संवेगानाम् intense, आसन्नः nearest, quick.

**Success (in Samadhi) is quick (for those), whose
(Vairagya) is intense.**

NOTES

Those who feel ardently for Self-realisation, who have burning Vairagya, attain at once to the state of Asamprajnata Samadhi. Burning Vairagya and intense Sadhana are needed. Then the fruit is near at hand. According to the degree of Vairagya and degree of Sadhana, there are nine stages or steps wherein Yogis halt. The fruit of Samprajnata Samadhi is. Asamprajnata Samadhi, and the fruit of Asamprajnata Samadhi is Kaivalya or absolute independence.

(4) Three kinds in Effort

मृदुमध्याधिमात्रत्वात्ततोऽपि विशेषः । I-22

मृदु mild, मध्य middling, moderate, अधिमात्र excessive, ततोऽपि further, विशेषः differentiation.

A further differentiation comes by mild, moderate or excessive (in efforts).

NOTES

The means are of three kinds, mild, medium and intense. Vairagya also is of three kinds, mild, middling and intense. Hence there are nine classes of Yogis. The fruit, Asamprajnata Samadhi, will directly be proportionate to the degree of means and Vairagya. Yogis are of mild, middling and intense energy and Vairagya by virtue of their habits of previous lives.

(5) By Destroyal of Samskaras and Isvara-pranidhana

(Sutras I-51 and II-45)

It is given in the Sutras I-51 that Samadhi will come by the destroyal of all Samskaras, and in Sutra II-45 by Isvara-pranidhana. The meaning of the Sutras and their notes are already given. Now I will pass on to the description of different kinds of Samadhi.

3. Dharmamegha Samadhi

प्रसंख्यानेऽप्यकुसीदस्य सर्वथा
विवेकख्यातेर्धर्ममेघः समाधिः । IV-29

प्रसंख्याने in the highest discriminative knowledge, अपि even, अकुसीदस्य having no interest left behind, सर्वथा विवेकख्यातेः constant discrimination, धर्ममेघः समाधिः Samadhi called the cloud of virtue.

Dharmamegha Samadhi or the Samadhi called the cloud of virtue, comes from constant discrimination, having no interest left in the highest discrimination.

NOTES

Even full discrimination is not the desired end. When the Yogi rejects the powers only, he gets the illumination Prasamkhyana or Dharmamegha. That Yogi who has understood the essence of 25 Tattvas and who has the discriminative knowledge between Prakriti and Purusha gets the power of knowing everything. He becomes the Lord of everything. When he has no attachment for this state also, he gets Viveka-khyati or full discrimination in the form of a continuous current at all places and in all conditions. This is 'cloud of virtue.' When the Yogi has renounced all powers, he gets the real knowledge, real peace and real strength of Purusha. He is full of bliss, purity and wisdom (Yathartha Jnana). He shines in his own native glory. He becomes ever free and independent. He who runs after Siddhis is still bound. Knowledge of the Truth or Purusha is far from him. Other thoughts which cause obstruction or breaks (*vide* Sutra IV-26), owing to past impressions, are not born now owing to the destruction of these impressions.

4. Benefits of Dharmamegha Samadhi

(1) Removal of Afflictions

ततः क्लेशकर्मनिवृत्तिः । IV-30

.ततः from that Samadhi, क्लेशकर्म of afflictions and Karmas, निवृत्तिः the removal.

From the Dharmamegha Samadhi comes the removal of all afflictions and Karmas.

NOTES

The cause for Samsara is Klesha-karmas that are mixed with Vasanas. When these are destroyed, the Yogi becomes free while living. There is no fear of downfall, as the Klesha-karmas, the seeds for Samsara are totally fried now. As this Samadhi showers always the state of Kaivalya, the fruit of actions that are called Akrishna and Asukla, it is called Dharmamegha. It is quite a significant name indeed. The afflictions and Karmas are already described in Sutras II-3, 15 & 16.

(2) Infinity of Knowledge

तदा सर्वावरणमलापेतस्य ज्ञानस्यानन्त्याज्ज्ञेयमल्पम् । IV-31

तदा then, सर्वावरणमलापेतस्य removal of all coverings of impurities, ज्ञानस्य knowledge, अनन्त्यात् due to infinity of, ज्ञेयम् knowable, अल्पम् very little.

Then comes the removal of all coverings of impurities due to the infinity of knowledge and the knowable becomes very little.

NOTES

When the Yogi gets this infinite knowledge, the knowledge that ordinary men get from worldly experiences and the knowable becomes very, very insignificant. The knowledge of the Yogi is like a sun. The knowledge of objects is like the light of a glow-worm. The Yogi sees without eyes, tastes without tongue, hears without ears, smells without nose and touches without skin. His Sankalpa can work miracles. He simply wills. Everything comes into being. This is described as follows: "The blind man pierced the pearl; the fingerless put a thread into it; the neckless wore it and the tongueless praised it"

(Taittiriya Aranyaka I-ii-5). The sum total of all knowledge of this world, of all other secular sciences is nothing, nothing, is mere husk when compared with the infinite knowledge of a Yogi who has attained Kaivalya.

(3) Gunas Come to an End

ततः कृतार्थानां परिणामक्रमसमाप्तिर्गुणानाम् । IV-32

ततः then, कृतार्थानाम् having fulfilled their part, परिणाम modifications, क्रम succession, समाप्ति end, गुणानाम् Gunas or qualities.

Then the succession of the modifications of Gunas comes to an end, having fulfilled their part.

NOTES

When the cloud of virtue dawns, when there is highest knowledge and when Para Vairagya fully manifests, the entire cessation of the effects of the three Gunas comes in. The Gunas operate for the enjoyment, experience and emancipation of the Purusha. The Purusha having realised His native state, the Gunas, of course, cease to act, they having fulfilled their end. Therefore the succession of the modifications of Gunas comes to an end for the Purusha who has attained Kaivalya.

(4) Simultaneous Knowledge

क्षणप्रतियोगी परिणामापरान्तनिर्ग्राह्यः क्रमः । IV-33

क्षणप्रतियोगी the uninterrupted sequence of moments, परिणामापरान्त cessation of modification, निर्ग्राह्यः cognised distinctly, क्रमः succession.

The succession is the uninterrupted sequence of moments distinctly cognised on the cessation of modification.

NOTES

Succession of moments implies order of time. Its form can only be understood if you have a knowledge of the minute particle of time Kshana. Succession is the uninterrupted flow of moments. It can be known only when a particular modification comes to an end. Succession has reference to order and time. For the Yogi who has attained Asamprajnata Samadhi, there is no succession for him. He has simultaneous knowledge. The past and future are blended in the present for him. Everything is 'now'. Everything is 'here'. He has transcended time and space.

5. Samprajnata Samadhi

(1) Definition

वितर्कविचारानन्दास्मितारूपानुगमात्सम्प्रज्ञातः । I-17

वितर्क argumentation, विचार deliberation, आनन्द happiness, अस्मिता egoism, रूप form, अनुगमात् accompanied by, सम्प्रज्ञातः Samprajnata Samadhi or concrete meditation.

Samprajnata Samadhi or concrete meditation is that which is accompanied by argumentation, deliberation, happiness, egoism and form.

NOTES

Samadhi is of two kinds viz., Samprajnata and Asamprajnata. Samprajnata Samadhi is the first step. In this Samadhi, Samskaras are not destroyed. This is also known as Sabija Samadhi, because the seeds or the Samskaras are there. In this there is Alambana or support.

In Samprajnata Samadhi there are four varieties viz., Savitarka, Savichara, Sananda and Asmita. All these will be explained in the subsequent Sutras. Samadhi can also be divided into two kinds, Sthula (gross) and Sukshma (subtle) that relates to Tanmatras and Indriyas. Samprajnata and Asamprajnata Samadhis are termed as Savikalpa and Nirvikalpa Samadhi by Vedantins and Bhaktas.

This Sutra refers actually to a series of meditations in an ascending order, first on the physical universe, then the subtle universe of potentials called Tanmatras, the cosmic complex known as space and time and cosmic Self sense

leading to a bliss born of pure consciousness. Though the
Sutra refers only to Vitarka, Vichara, Ananda and Asmita,
they are further capable of categorisation as involved in
space-time consciousness or not involved in space-time
consciousness. These stages are intricate and cannot be
understood by merely a study of books.

(2) Savitarka Samadhi

तत्र शब्दार्थज्ञानविकल्पैः संकीर्णा सवितर्का समापत्तिः । I-42

तत्र there, शब्दार्थज्ञान word, meaning and understanding,
विकल्पैः options, संकीर्णा confused, सवितर्का with argumentation, समापत्तिः thought transformation or concentration.

**There the concentration in which the options of word,
meaning and understanding are confused is called Savitarka
Samadhi or the Samadhi with argumentation.**

NOTES

If you concentrate and meditate on the gross objects,
on their nature and in relation to time and space, it is
Savitarka Samadhi (Samadhi with argumentation). It is
Sthula Dhyana. You will get control over the object. You
will acquire full knowledge of the object. You will get
psychic powers (Siddhis).

The 'cow ' as a word, the 'cow' as an object and the
'cow' as an idea, though different from one another, are
cognised as indistinct. You begin to analyse. The
characteristics of the word are different; the characteristics
of the idea are different; and the characteristics of the
object are also different. Everything has a name which has
some meaning. When the mind apprehends a word and
meditates on its meaning and form as well as on the
understanding of both, and thus lose itself in the thing
completely, it is called Savitarka Samadhi. Sound causes
vibration in the mind. It is carried through the external
auditory meatus (external opening of the ear), through the
auditory nerve to the auditory centre of the brain. Now a

reaction takes place. The mind reacts. It understands the meaning of the sound. Now knowledge manifests. Now comes perception or cognition of the object. The mixture of these three, sound, meaning and knowledge constitute perception or cognition of an object. It is Savitarka Samadhi.

(3) Savichara Samadhi

If you meditate on the subtle Tanmatras, on their nature and in relation to time and space, it is Savichara Samadhi (Samadhi with deliberation). This is Sukshma Dhyana. You will get knowledge of the Tanmatras. You will have great control over Tanmatras. Savitarka, Nirvitarka, Savichara and Nirvichara are called Grahya Samapatti.

(4) Sananda Samadhi

If you give up the gross and the subtle elements, if you fix the Indriyas in their respective places and if you give up the gross and the subtle meditation, and if you meditate on the Sattvic mind itself, it is known as Sananda Samadhi. This is called Grahya Samapatti, cognition of the instrument of cognition.

(5) Asmita Samadhi

When the Sattvic ego only remains during deep meditation, is called Asmita Samadhi. There is only Prajna of 'Aham-Tvam' in this Samadhi. The Yogi who has reached this stage is a Videha (without body). Prakriti-layas are those who in this state get themselves merged in nature. You will have to proceed further if you want Kaivalya. This is called as Grahitri Samapatti, cognition of the knower.

Savitarka is gross Samadhi. Savichara is subtle Samadhi. Sananda is deep subtle Samadhi. Asmita is still more deep subtle Samadhi. These are all stages like the steps of an ascending stair-case.

(6) Sabija Samadhi

ता एव सबीजः समाधिः । I-46

ता these (Savitarka, Savichara, Sananda and Asmita Samadhis), एव only, सबीजः with seed, समाधिः Samadhi.

These only, viz., Savitarka, Savichara Sananda and Asmita are Sabija Samadhi or Samadhi with seed (Samskaras).

NOTES

The seeds are the Samskaras of past actions which give birth and death. These meditations cannot give full security. They cannot ensure final liberation, as the seeds are not fried or destroyed. They have got Alambana (support) on external objects, gross or subtle. Niralambana, Nirbija Samadhi only can give the final salvation.

6. Asamprajnata Samadhi

(1) Stopping Mental Modifications

विरामप्रत्ययाभ्यासपूर्वः संस्कारशेषोऽन्यः । I-18

विराम cessation, प्रत्ययाभ्यास by the constant practice, पूर्वः the former, संस्कारशेष in which the impressions only remain, अन्यः the other.

The other Samadhi is that which consists only of impressions being brought about by the constant practice of the cessation of mental modifications.

NOTES

This is the highest Asamprajnata Samadhi which brings Kaivalya or Independence. Here there is no Alambana for the mind. It is rendered perfectly steady. All Samskaras are fried up.

There is no Triputi here. This is not the Laya state or deep sleep. There is perfect awareness. This is a stage where a Yogi gets the highest knowledge. There is Prajna or pure consciousness. This is the state like ocean without waves. The only Sadhana for attaining this state is Para

Vairagya. Rajas and Tamas are completely destroyed.
When there is Ekagrata, Samprajnata Samadhi is possible.
Asamprajnata Samadhi is possible when there is perfect
Nirodha of mind. Para Vairagya brings complete rest to the
mind. All Vrittis stop. This is the highest end of Raja Yoga
which gives freedom.

In Samprajnata Samadhi there is only a partial
inhibition of mental functions. Partial inhibition of the
mental functions cannot totally uproot the seeds of rebirth.
It cannot lead to final liberation wherein the seer rests in
his own native, pristine, Divine Glory. Asamprajnata
Samadhi destroys the impressions of all antecedent mental
functions, and even goes so far as to tide over even
Prarabdha. A Yogi has no Prarabdha at all. The mind
having no object to grasp, becomes as it were, non-existent.
This is Nirbija or Niralambana Samadhi.

(2) Nirvichara Samadhi

स्मृतिपरिशुद्धौ स्वरूपशून्येवार्थमात्रनिर्भासा निर्वितर्का । I-43

स्मृति memory, परिशुद्धौ on the purification, स्वरूप its own
nature, शून्य devoid of, इव it were, अर्थमात्र the object alone,
निर्भासा shining, निर्वितर्का Nirvitarka Samadhi or the Samadhi
without argumentation.

**Nirvitarka Samadhi is that in which the mind shines as
the object alone on the disappearance of memory and when
the mind is, as it were, devoid of its own nature.**

NOTES

You have seen the different kinds of Samprajnata
Samadhi. Among those gross forms of meditation, if you
meditate by taking the elements out of time and space, and
by thinking on them as they are, it will become Nirvitarka
Samadhi (without argumentation). This is a higher form of
Samadhi than the previous one. Everything besides the
complete idea of the object is forgotten in this Samadhi.
The mind is not conscious of name, form, meaning or

relation of the object. It is absorbed in one idea. The
faculty of memory is suppressed here as it brings
association of name, form, meaning, relation, etc. In
ordinary persons, it is difficult to separate the sound,
meaning and the knowledge, as they occur with great
rapidity. A Yogi who practises Nirvitarka Samadhi will be
able to distinguish clearly one from the other. The state
described in this Sutra is perfect Nirvitarka Samadhi. The
mind of the Yogi becomes very, very subtle on account of
various practices in concentration and the development of
qualities like Maitri, Karuna and Mudita. The disturbing
Rajas and Tamas have been wiped out.

(3) Nirvichara and Subtle Objects

एतयैव सविचारा निर्विचारा च सूक्ष्मविषया व्याख्याता । I-44

एतया by this, एव also, सविचारा with deliberation, निर्विचारा
without deliberation, च and, सूक्ष्म subtle, विषया for objects,
व्याख्याता are explained.

**By this (process) meditation with deliberation and without
deliberation with their objects as subtle, are also explained.**

NOTES

Just as the two kinds of argumentative concentration
refer to the gross elements, so the two kinds of
concentration with deliberation and without deliberation
refer to subtle elements. Sananda and Sasmita are also
included here. Vichara here means 'meditative state.' It is
not the Tarka Vichara.

(4) The Province of Subtle objects

सूक्ष्मविषयत्वं चालिङ्गपर्यवसानम् । I-45

सूक्ष्मविषयत्वम् the province of the subtle (objects), च and,
अलिङ्गपर्यवसानम् upto noumenal extremity or Mula Prakriti.

**The province of the subtle objects reach upto (or end with)
Mula Prakriti.**

NOTES

Behind all subtle objects is Mula Prakriti, the primal cause. Pradhana is a terminology of the Sankhyas for Mula Prakriti. It means the 'chief'. The other principles, Mahat, Ahamkara, Manas, Tanmatras and the gross elements are derived from this. Hence it has got this significant name. Vedantins call this 'Avyaktam' (unmanifested), 'Avyakritam' (undifferentiated), because the matter and energy are one here. They are not differentiated. All kinds of sounds also exist here in an undifferentiated state. Hence the significant name 'undifferentiated.' All the products or Vikritis are dissolved at the end of Pralaya in the chief Pradhana. When the three Gunas are in a state of equilibrium in Pralaya, the name Prakriti is given. This is the Gunasamya Avastha. When the equilibrium is disturbed during Srishti, the state of Vaishamya Avastha begins. Then this motion of Jivas is set up through the influence of Sattva, Rajas and Tamas. One who has mastered the four stages of concentration described above, gets mastery over Pradhana. Purusha, which is more subtle than Pradhana, is above Pradhana. He is only the instrumental cause for this world (Nimitta Karana). Mula Prakriti is Upadhana Karana or material cause for this world. Pradhana is also known by the name 'Alinga.' This means without mark. The Sukshma state of gross elements is Tanmatras. Mahat is more subtle than the Tanmatras. Mahat is individual Buddhi Tattva. It is also known by the name 'Linga.' Pradhana is more subtle than the Mahat.

7. Benefits of Nirvichara Samadhi

(1) Internal Peace

निर्विचारवैशारद्येऽध्यात्मप्रसादः । I-47

निर्विचार without meditation, वैशारद्ये when purified, अध्यात्म spiritual, प्रसादः peace of mind.

When the meditation without deliberation is purified, comes the spiritual internal peace of mind.

NOTES

As there is pure Sattva only in the mind, owing to the eradication of Rajas and Tamas, there is light and purity in the mind. The mind is perfectly steady. So, there is Prasada or contentment and peace of mind or subjective luminosity. The Purusha, who is all-bliss, all-knowledge, all-purity can only be realised when the mind is perfectly steady and is filled with purity. The Yogi gets simultaneous knowledge of everything.

If you want to meditate on the subtle Tanmatras by taking them out of time and space by thinking as they are, it will constitute Nirvichara Samadhi (Samadhi without deliberation).

(2) Ritambara Prajna

ऋतम्भरा तत्र प्रज्ञा । I-48

ऋतम्भरा full of Truth, तत्र therein, प्रज्ञा Consciousness.

The consciousness therein is full of Truth.

NOTES

There is the real knowledge free from Samsaya (doubt) and Vipareeta Bhavanas (perverted knowledge). There is knowledge by mere intuition. The real essence is revealed here. There is not even a trace of false knowledge. Worldly knowledge, knowledge from books is only false knowledge.

(3) The Range of Intellect

श्रुतानुमानप्रज्ञाभ्यामन्यविषया विशेषार्थत्वात् । I-49

श्रुत revelation, अनुमान inferential, प्रज्ञाभ्याम् from those of cognition, अन्य different, विषया object, विशेषार्थत्वात् due to reference to particulars.

The range of intellect is different from those of revelation and inferential cognition.

NOTES

Its subject is different from testimony and inference, for, it refers to particulars (which cannot be reached by testimony and inference), i.e., ordinary knowledge. Ritambara is a special Jnana Bhumika. You get Yadartha Jnana or real wisdom. In this state of Prajna, knowledge of Parama Anus, knowledge of hidden things and distant objects is directly obtained. This knowledge is perfectly true and is absolutely free from errors. Knowledge of minute particulars is obtained. Reason has got its own limitations. It is an imperfect instrument. It cannot solve many problems of life. A man of lower reasoning power can be defeated by a man of higher reasoning power. It cannot answer the 'Why?' of the Universe. The very word 'mystery' admits that reason has not got the power to explain certain things. It shines in borrowed light from the Purusha. It takes you to the threshold of intuition and leaves you there. It helps in a way. Intuition transcends reason but does not contradict reason. The Yogi gets supersensual knowledge and knowledge that lies beyond reason through intuition.

(4) Samskaras Are Obstructed

तज्जः संस्कारोऽन्यसंस्कारप्रतिबन्धी । I-50

तज्जः therefrom, संस्कारः impression, अन्य other, संस्कार impressions, प्रतिबन्धी obstruct.

The impressions therefrom (from the Samadhi previously described), obstruct other impressions.

NOTES

The impression on the mind produced by this Samadhi prevents other impressions from gaining ground on it. The mind has become absolutely pure now. This Samadhi has the power to suppress all the old Vishaya Samskaras. Samskaras are your real enemies. Samskaras constitute the destiny of man. During concentration, they all join together and attack you with great vehemence. But the Samskara of this Samadhi comes to your rescue. It destroys all the other vicious Samskaras. It is a great asset for you. The mind is absolutely steady now. It can never run towards objects.

(5) Nirbija Samadhi

तस्यापि निरोधे सर्वनिरोधान्निर्बीजः समाधिः । I-51

तस्यापि निरोधे by the suppression of even that (Samskara), सर्वनिरोधात् due to the suppression of all (Samskaras), निर्बीजः समाधिः Nirbija (seedless) Samadhi.

By the suppression of that Samskara (the Samadhi Samskara) also, due to the suppression of all Samskaras, comes the Nirbija Samadhi.

NOTES

When the Samskara caused by the experience of Ritambara Prajna is also restrained, all other Samskaras also are totally restrained. Now all the seeds are totally burnt up in the fire of Asamprajnata Samadhi. In the beginning there were countless Vrittis. These were all controlled gradually. There was only one Vritti. In this state, there was the state of 'I am'. There was 'Aham Prajna'. This Vritti also is given up. Then the Kaivalya state is reached. The Yogi who has attained Kaivalya is called a Mukta. The mind, thus having nothing to rest upon, is destroyed by itself (Mano-nasa). Purusha alone shines in perfect bliss, knowledge, peace and glory. The Yogi is absolutely free. He realises his real Immortal nature.

(6) The State of Videhas

भवप्रत्ययो विदेहप्रकृतिलयानाम् । I-19

भवप्रत्ययो the cause of the concrete universe, विदेहप्रकृति- लयानाम् Videhas and Prakriti-layas who are merged in Prakriti (nature).

This (Asamprajnata Samadhi) gives the state of Videhas and Prakriti-layas who are merged in nature.

NOTES

Videhas and Prakriti-layas are inferior Yogis who have not finished the complete ascent in the Yogic ladder. They have not reached the final goal of Yoga. They have stopped at some stage. Videhas and Prakriti-layas are distinct from each other.

Videhas do not feel the physical body, but they feel that they have a very subtle body. The minds of Prakriti-layas have not yet fulfilled the object of their existence; they have still work before them. Prakriti-layas having their minds merged in the Prakriti, with its work still undone, enjoy a state of something like absolute freedom, as long as they do not come back by virtue of the work yet to be done.

Pratyaya means cause. The artificial, abstract meditation or Asamprajnata Samadhi is that in which the meditation is brought about in this very world by methods or means prescribed in the scriptures such as Sraddha, power, memory, Prajna, meditation, etc. This is Upaya-pratyaya.

In the natural, Bhava-pratyaya, Asamprajnata Samadhi, discernment, non-attachment come by themselves without any practice in this birth on account of the practices in the previous birth. By mere willing, the Yogi enters into Asamprajnata Samadhi. You will find in Gita a description of Yoga Bhrashtas: "Having attained to the worlds of the pure doing, and having dwelt there for immemorial years, he who fell from Yoga is reborn in a pure and blessed house. Or he may even be born in a family of wise Yogis; but such a birth as that is most difficult to obtain in this world. There he recovereth the characteristics belonging to his former body, and with these he again laboureth for perfection."

Bhava-pratyaya or natural Samadhi is only possible in the case of Videhas and Prakriti-layas. Ordinary persons should adopt the means and acquire discernment, non-attachment, etc. The mind, having all its functions duly performed, becomes completely absorbed into its root cause along with the Prarabdha and the Samskaras of inhibition. This is the highest Yoga which brings Kaivalya.

Videhas and Prakriti-layas are born again in this world. Although the mind in Prakriti-layas has become similar to the Prakriti, yet they come back when the limit has been reached. As on the cessation of the rainy season, the body of the frog is assimilated to the earth and comes back to life again on coming into contact with rain water so does the mind of the Prakriti-laya. It is only the full-blown Yogi, who has reached the highest Asamprajnata Samadhi and in whom all the Samskaras are fried, will not be born again.

8. Instructions on Samadhi

1. Samadhi is not like a stone-like inert state as many foolish persons imagine. When the self is bound down to its empirical accidents, its activities are not fully exercised, and when the limitations of the empirical existence are transcended the universal life is identified and you have enrichment of the self. You will have a rich inner life. You will have an expanded cosmic life and supra-cosmic life too.

2. Intuition is a spiritual Anubhava. It is direct perception or immediate knowledge through Samadhi. Professor Bergsen of France preaches about intuition to make the people understand that there is another higher source of knowledge than intellect. In intuition there is no reasoning process at all. It is Pratyaksha. Intuition transcends reason but does not contradict it. Intellect takes a man to the door of intuition and returns back. Intuition is Divya Drishti. It is Jnana-Chakshu. Spiritual flashes and

glimpses of Truth come through intuition. Inspiration, revelation, spiritual insight come through intuition.

3. A sudden stroke of mystic illumination puts an end to all the empirical existence altogether and the very idea or remembrance of such a thing as this world absolutely leaves the self.

4. Samadhi is of two kinds viz., Jada Samadhi and Chaitanya Samadhi. A Hatha Yogi, through the practice of Khechari Mudra, can shut himself in a box which is buried underneath the ground for months and years. There is no supersensual knowledge in this kind of Samadhi. In Chaitanya Samadhi, there is perfect awareness. The Yogi comes down with new, supersensuous wisdom.

5. A Hatha Yogi draws all his Prana from the different parts of his body and takes it to the Sahasrara Chakra at the top of the head. Then he enters into Samadhi. Therefore it is very difficult to bring him down to objective consciousness by merely shaking his body. Hatha Yogis have remained buried underneath the earth in Samadhi for thousands of years. They plug the posterior nostrils through Khechari Mudra with their tongue. You can bring down to normal objective consciousness a Raja Yogi or a Bhakta or a Jnana Yogi by mere shaking of the body or blowing a conch. Queen Chudalai brought down her husband Sikhidhvaja from Samadhi by shaking his body. Lord Hari brought Prahlada down from his Samadhi by blowing His conch.

6. A Bhakta gets Bhava Samadhi through Prema of the Lord. A Raja Yogi gets Asamprajnata Samadhi through Chitta Vritti Nirodha, by suppressing the mental modifications. A Vedantin gets Samadhi through Mithyatva Buddhi and concentration on the idea of Asti-Bhati-Priya (the Anvaya method).

7. When the Yogi has reached the last perfect stage of meditation and Samadhi, the fire whereof burns all the

residue of his actions. He at once gets liberation in this very life (Jivanmukti).

8. During sleep you rest in Sat-chit-ananda Atman or pure consciousness and enjoy the spiritual bliss which is independent of objects. The difference between sleep and Samadhi is that, in sleep there is the veil of ignorance. When you come down from Samadhi you come with new spiritual knowledge.

9. If there is a mind, there is the world also. If you can produce Mano-nasa consciously through Sadhana by getting rid of this little 'I' and 'mineness', this world will disappear.

10. The Yogi ascends the various rungs of the Yogic ladder, stage by stage and acquires different experiences, knowledge and powers. He first gets Savitarka and Nirvitarka Samadhi. He then enters Savichara and Nirvichara Samadhi. Then he experiences Sananda and Sasmita Samadhi.

CHAPTER XIV

KAIVALYA

1. What Is Kaivalya

पुरुषार्थशून्यानां गुणानां प्रतिप्रसवः कैवल्यं स्वरूपप्रतिष्ठा वा
चितिशक्तिरिति । IV-34

पुरुषार्थशून्यानाम् devoid of motives, गुणानाम् of the qualities,
प्रतिप्रसवः become latent, कैवल्यम् Kaivalya or perfect
independence, स्वरूप its own nature, प्रतिष्ठा established, वा
or, चितिशक्तिः the power of consciousness, इति thus.

**Kaivalya (perfect independence) comes when the Gunas
(qualities), devoid of motive, become latent. Or the power of
consciousness gets established in its own nature.**

NOTES

The Gunas act for the enjoyment of the Purusha. As
soon as the Purusha realises His own native state of
isolation, the Gunas, having fulfilled the object, cease to
act. Their effects, the various modifications of Gunas, get
Laya or involution. They merge into their causes. Nothing
remains for the Purusha to cognise. This does not mean
that the universe has come to an end. The world continues
to exist as usual for those who have not attained Kaivalya.
The Indriyas are drawn into the mind, the mind into the
Mahat, and the Mahat into the Purusha.

2. Means for Kaivalya

सत्त्वपुरुषयोः शुद्धिसाम्ये कैवल्यमिति । III-56

सत्त्वपुरुषयोः Sattva and Purusha, शुद्धि purity, साम्ये equality,
कैवल्यम् Kaivalya (perfect independence), इति thus.

(178)

On the equality of purity between Purusha and Sattva comes Kaivalya (perfect independence).

NOTES

Perfection is attained when the intellect becomes as pure as the Atman itself. When the soul realises that it is absolutely independent and it does not depend on anything else in this world, this highest knowledge, Kaivalya, Isolation or perfect independence comes in. The soul feels that it is ever free, unchanging, immortal, beginningless, endless, infinite, beyond time, space and causation, full of bliss, peace and knowledge. When the intellect or Sattva is rendered as pure as the Purusha, when it loses all consciousness of action on its own part, then its purity is said to be equal to that of the Purusha. The intellect or Sattva is annihilated. Purusha only remains free in His native, pristine divine glory. 'Sattva' means here intellect. Purusha is reflected in intellect. Sattva is the cause for knowledge and Ahamkara. The intellect attains the same state as that of Purusha when it becomes absolutely pure and when it remains motionless and when all its functions and activities stop completely. In Sutra II-25 another means for Kaivalya is given.

3. Purusha Cognises Through Intellect

द्रष्टा दृशिमात्रः शुद्धोऽपि प्रत्ययानुपश्यः । II-20

द्रष्टा the seer, दृशिमात्रः intelligence only, शुद्ध-अपि even though pure, प्रत्यय by mental effort, through intellect, अनुपश्यः cognise, see.

Though the seer is pure intelligence only, he cognises ideas through intellect.

NOTES

The Purusha is an embodiment of intelligence. He is ever pure and eternally free. He is always the silent witness of the play of Prakriti. Through intellect, the Purusha appears as if seeing, although really he never sees or does anything.

The qualities of intellect are superimposed on the Purusha. Just as the real colour of the flower appears on the transparent crystal, so also the qualities of Buddhi appear on the Purusha. Hence, the Purusha appears to be happy or miserable.

4. Knowable Is for the Purusha

तदर्थ एव दृश्यस्यांत्मा । II-21

तदर्थ for His (Purusha) purpose, एव only, दृश्यस्य knowable, आत्मा existence.

For His (Purusha's) purpose only is the existence of the knowable (the object of experience).

NOTES

If the Purusha were not, the being of Prakriti could never have been as stated in Sutra II-18. Just as the cows allow the milk to flow freely to the calf, so also this Prakriti places all her products before the Purusha for his enjoyment, experience and emancipation.

5. Pradhana Is Not Destroyed

कृतार्थ प्रति नष्टमप्यनष्टं तदन्यसाधारणत्वात् । II-22

कृतार्थम् whose purpose has been fulfilled, प्रति to him, नष्टम् destroyed, अपि even though, अनष्टम् not destroyed, तद् from that, अन्य others, साधारणत्वात् common.

Even though destroyed to him, whose purpose has been fulfilled, it (Pradhana) is not yet destroyed, because it is common to others.

NOTES

According to the Sankhya and Raja Yoga philosophy, even if one becomes a Mukta, the Pradhana and its modifications exist for others.

6. Samyoga Explained

स्वस्वामिशक्त्योः स्वरूपोपलब्धिहेतुः संयोगः । II-23

स्व being owned (nature, Drishya), स्वामि of owning (the Lord), शक्त्योः of their powers, स्वरूप of the natures, उपलब्धि recognition, हेतु cause, संयोगः junction.

The junction is the cause for the recognition of the powers of nature and its Lord.

NOTES

The Purusha unites with the Buddhi and enjoys the different objects. This is the cause for human sufferings. Ignorance is the cause for this conjunction. This Prakriti and Purusha are united from time immemorial. If this union is separated, the Purusha recognises his original, divine glory. The original conjunction is the union of Purusha with the Buddhi. Through Buddhi, he is united with body.

He mistakes this perishable body for the real Purusha. Through this body, he gets united with wife, children, relatives and friends. The whole Samsara has started now. Disconnect yourself from the Prakriti and become a Mukta Purusha. This is the essential teaching of Raja Yoga.

7. Mind Is Not Purusha

विशेषदर्शिन आत्मभावभावनाविनिवृत्तिः । IV-25

विशेषदर्शिन for the man of discrimination, आत्म the Self or Purusha, भावभावना the perception of the mind, विनिवृत्तिः ceases.

The perception of the mind as Purusha ceases for the man of discrimination.

NOTES

Just as the existence of seeds is inferred from the blades of grass shooting forth in the rainy season, so also it is rightly inferred that he whose tears flow (Asrupatha) and whose hairs stand on end (Pulaka) when he hears the name of God or Moksha, has surely a store of Karma tending to liberation, as the seed of the recognition of the distinction is already there. The perception of mind ceases to appear as Purusha.

8. Discrimination Is Sevenfold

तस्य सप्तधा प्रान्तभूमिः प्रज्ञा । II-27

तस्य his (the Yogi of unbroken discrimination), प्रज्ञा discrimination, सप्तधा sevenfold, प्रान्तभूमिः at the final stage.

His (the Yogi of unbroken discrimination) discrimination is sevenfold at the final stage.

NOTES

The Yogi gets the knowledge in seven grades one after another. The seven grades are the seven Jnana Bhumikas. The first four relate to the objective side and the next three to the subjective side. In each Bhumika, he has the followings feelings:

(1) "I have known all that was to be known and nothing further remains to know. The dissatisfied state of mind has disappeared. All doubts vanish."

(2) "Nothing can give me any pain."

(3) "By attaining Kaivalya, I have attained everything and nothing more remains." (Here he is an Aptakama).

(4) "I have fulfilled all my duties now." (Here he is a Krita-kritya).

(5) "My mind is at complete rest. All distractions have vanished." (Here the freedom of the mind is threefold).

(6) "The Gunas have all dropped away, like stones from the mountain-top, never to rise up again."

(7) "I am what I am, ever free. I am established in my Self. I am all bliss and knowledge. I have no connections. I am Kevala Purusha."

These are the seven stages of knowledge or feelings of the Yogi in the seven Jnana Bhumikas.

9. Mind Fit for Kaivalya

तदा विवेकनिम्नं कैवल्यप्राग्भारं चित्तम् । IV-26

तदा then, विवेकनिम्नम् bent towards discrimination, कैवल्य Kaivalya, प्राग्भारम् is attracted towards, चित्तम् mind.

Then the mind is bent towards discrimination, and is attracted towards Kaivalya.

NOTES

The mind which was bent upon worldly things is now bent upon discrimination. Such a mind is naturally attracted towards Kaivalya. The Yogi has no other thought than the idea of Kaivalya. He now knows that the mind or Prakriti is entirely distinct from the Soul or Purusha. He becomes absolutely fearless. All sorrows melt now. All Klesas totally vanish. He feels his absolute freedom now. He has reached the highest goal of life. He has the highest knowledge.

10. Thoughts Are Obstacles

तच्छिद्रेषु प्रत्ययान्तराणि संस्कारेभ्यः । IV-27

तच्छिद्रेषु in the intervals, प्रत्ययान्तराणि arise other thoughts, संस्कारेभ्यः from the old Samskaras or impressions.

In the intervals, arise other thoughts from the old Samskaras.

NOTES

Even though the mind of the Yogi is full of the idea of Kaivalya, at intervals the previous Samskaras overpower him. There comes break in his knowledge. All these Samskaras also should be obliterated or entirely wiped out. Then he will have continuous knowledge without any break. This is the meaning of this Sutra. In the interval between one Vritti and another Vritti, extraneous Vrittis born of Purva Vasanas may try to enter as foreign bodies and may break the continuous stream of discrimination and Kaivalya.

11. Remedy for Obstacles

हानमेषां क्लेशवदुक्तम् । IV-28

हानम् destruction, एषाम् their (old Vasanas), क्लेशवत् like the afflictions, उक्तम् is described.

Their (old Vasanas) destruction is by destroying like the afflictions (described in Sutra II-10).

NOTES

The Vrittis that manifest in the internal, lose their force and energy gradually and become like burnt seeds and so do not trouble the Yogi. The old Vasanas should be completely destroyed by the same way as the afflictions are destroyed, i.e., by meditation and by resolving the mind back into its primal cause, i.e., by attaining Samadhi.

Kaivalya is not a state of negation or annihilation as some foolishly imagine. It is perfect awareness. It is like Amalaka fruit in the palm of the hand. It is the highest state of bliss and knowledge. It is the highest goal of life. It is the eternal life in the spirit or pure consciousness. It is the state of absolute peace, where cares, worries, fears, anxieties, tribulations, sorrows, Vasanas and Trishnas do not torment the soul. It is the state of eternal sunshine and perennial joy. It is a state that cannot be adequately described in words. How can you describe the sweetness of sugarcandy? It is the state which is to be realised and felt through Aparoksha-anubhuti, one's own experience through Vairagya, Sadhana and Samadhi.

When the Purusha has completely disconnected himself from the Prakriti and its effects, when he has realised that his happiness does not depend upon external objects, when he has recognised his own glory and independence, and when he feels his absolute freedom, then alone he has attained Kaivalya.

The Purusha realises His own native state of Divine Glory, Isolation or Absolute Independence. He has completely disconnected himself from the Prakriti and its effects. He feels his absolute freedom and attains Kaivalya, the highest goal of Raja Yoga. All Klesha-karmas are destroyed now. The Gunas having fulfilled their objects of Bhoga and Apavarga now entirely cease to act. He has simultaneous knowledge now. The past and future are blended into the present. Everything is 'now'. The sum total of all knowledge of the three worlds, of all secular sciences is nothing, nothing; it is mere husk when compared to the infinite knowledge of a Yogi who has attained Kaivalya. Glory, glory to such exalted Yogins. May their blessings be upon us all!

Om Santi Santi Santih!

ॐ

EPILOGUE

Dear Readers! You have now a comprehensive and an intelligent understanding of the mind, its nature, qualities and functioning of and the different ways of its control. Mere understanding itself will not serve the purpose much. What is wanted, what is seriously expected of you all is constant, intense, sustained, solid Sadhana for Self-realisation and the attainment of Kaivalya. Yoga is not for the idle, talkative people. It is for sincere, earnest students who have understood the magnitude of human sufferings in this phenomenal world and who are really thirsting for union with God and for deliverance from this Samsara. Yoga demands and will continue to demand from you knack, aptitude, vigilance, patience, perseverance, dispassion and steady, regular Abhyasa.

Theory precedes practice. Mere theory alone cannot help you in enjoying the fruits of Yoga. You will have to put the theory into daily practice. Mere intellectual curiosity, temporary juvenile enthusiasm and emotional bubbling cannot help you at all in any way in Yoga. Mere posing 'I am a Yogi' by cramming a few Sutras of Yoga Darsana is nothing but downright hypocrisy and wholesale swindling. Yoga is not meant to make one's living comfortable. Yoga is not a commercial business. To cheat God and your own self and the public by some false demonstrations in some Yogic practices is a heinous capital crime. To cheat others in the name of religion is abominable. This deserves maximum punishment. There is no Prayaschitta or expiatory rites for this deception.

How patiently and cautiously the fisherman watches the bait to catch a single fish! How energetically and

(186)

untiringly a student works for passing his M.Sc. Examination! How vigilant is the man who wants to catch the train at 2 a.m.! How smart and careful is the surgeon in the operation theatre when the patient is on the table! How alert is the lawyer when he is arguing the case in the sessions! How vigilant is the captain of a steamer when there is a cyclone or iceberg! Even so, you will have to work hard in the practice of Yoga if you care to realise fully the fruits of Yoga and Asamprajnata Samadhi.

Now then, stand up friends. Plod on. Push on in your practice. Be true and sincere. Practice the different limbs Yama, Niyama, Asana, Pranayama, Pratyahara, Dharana, Dhyana and Samadhi carefully. Become an expert in each step. I again remind you: Care not for the Siddhis. Be not troubled, be not anxious if there is a little delay in your progress and advancement. You will have to thoroughly regenerate, overhaul the old Samskaras and fight with the Klesas and Indriyas. Have full trust in Isvara and the teachings of Raja Yoga philosophy. Destroy the doubts and desires in the burning ground of the mind by the fire of discrimination. If you can afford, move to a cool place during summer for keeping up the continuity of practice. Become a Raja Yogi and disseminate the knowledge of Rishi Patanjali far and wide after full realisation.

Our cordial prostrations and salutations to our Universal Mother Nature, Prakriti or Pradhana! How kind, merciful and patient She is! How many varieties of fruits, grains, edibles, jewels, clothes, rivers, sun, moon and stars, etc., She has created for the enjoyment of these little souls! She always stands invisible by the side of Her children day and night, rocks the cradle, feeds, clothes, nurses and attends on them with untiring energy and patience, watches their actions and gives lessons through the experiences of this world and helps them to evolve quickly. Pain and sufferings are Her blessings in disguise for the uplift of the souls. Eventually She takes the Jiva to the

Lord Purusha, and bestows on him the state Kaivalya. Let us once more salute our Mother, with folded hands, whose Grace alone enables one to cross this ocean of Samsara.

May Joy, bliss, immortality, Kaivalya abide with you for ever!

May God bestow on you health and strength to control the mind!

May Asamprajnata Samadhi be the Goal of your life!

May the blessings of Lord Siva, Krishna be upon you all!

Glory to all the exalted Yogins!

ॐ पूर्णमदः पूर्णमिदं पूर्णात्पूर्णमुदच्यते ।
पूर्णस्य पूर्णमादाय पूर्णमेवावशिष्यते ॥

ॐ शान्ति शान्ति शान्तिः ।

Sivananda

RISHIKESH
15th November, 1936

GLEANINGS

(From Different Sources)

1. General

Having studied all the Sastras and having pondered over them well again and again, this Yoga Sastra has been found to be the only true and firm doctrine.

The person who has control over himself attains verily success through faith; none other can succeed. Therefore, Yoga should be practised with faith, care and perseverance.

To the ignorant, the express significance (of the Vedas) is like a thing sunk in mire. It is like the howling of a dog with its eye cast up in the heavens.

Persons who stroll through a bazaar street without any longing for the things therein are like those who have sojourned therein. Similarly to persons in full spiritual beatitude, cities and woods will constitute no difference.

Through Sanga (attraction of the mind), material objects are caused; through it, all accidents are generated; through it, all desires arise; through it this mundane existence arises. Therefore, it is the renunciation of this Sanga that is said to be Moksha.

The mind should think of the Paramatman with whom Union is sought through the path of Yoga comprising Yama, etc., or through logical analysis or through the worship and meditation etc., of Me—but by no other means.

So long as the self is related to the body, the organs and Pranas, relative existence, even though unreal, has a semblance of reality for the undiscriminating man.

2. Yama and Niyama

Non-injury, truthfulness, freedom from theft, lust, anger and greed, and an effort to do what is agreeable and beneficial to all beings — this is common duty of all castes.

The man of self-control should avoid from a safe distance the company of women as well as of those who associate with the latter, sit in a secluded and congenial place, and ever alert think of Me.

No other association causes so much misery and bondage as that of women and those that associate with them.

The man of uncontrolled senses, seeing women — the enchantment — created by Lord and being tempted by their blandishments, falls into abysmal darkness, like the moth into the fire.

Control speech, control mind, control the Pranas and organs; control also the impure intellect by the purified intellect. Then you will no more return to the world.

Yama and Niyama, if rightly practised by men, surely produce results (liberation or material prosperity) according to their desires.

3. Asana

Conquering posture and (through that) controlling the breath, one, ever alert, should collect the mind together and hold it steady through renunciation and systematic practice.

Being firm in the unshaken (spiritual) wisdom constitutes Asana.

4. Pranayama

There are two means of Yoga to avert the dire melting pains of existence. The two means, viz., true Jnana and control of Prana should, rightly speaking, be classed under Yoga; yet in ordinary usage, the control of Prana alone is called Yoga.

Having, through a study of Atma Jnana books, initiated oneself into the good graces of a Guru, after a ceaseless practice of Vairagya and liberation from the trammels of Samsara, if one is filled with non-desires and Brahmic meditation, then through the means adapted for the control of Prana, it will be controlled.

Through a long practice of Prana's control and through the initiations by a Guru, Asana, diet and Dhyana, Prana is controlled.

The wise say that the beneficent control of Prana leads to that of the mind, and causes in one equality of vision over all. It generates happiness and will not in the least allow sensual objects to arise in the mind.

5. Control of mind

A mental wave is never produced by anything that has not been seen or heard of. So the mind of a man who controls his senses is gradually stilled and is perfectly at peace.

It is not possible on the part of the one-thoughted to control the mind by sitting up again and again except through the approved means. In the matter of the control of the mind, the effective means are the attainment of spiritual knowledge, association with the wise, the entire abdication of all Vasanas and the control of Pranas.

A stainless mind without attractions though engaged in the worldly acts, will never be bound thereby. A mind with attractions, though engaged in innumerable Tapas will ever be in bondage.

No power is beyond the reach of the sage who has controlled his mind, senses, nerve-currents and disposition and concentrates on Me.

Those Yogins, who are able to control Prana and (therefore) arrest the mind both internally and externally, fly to a great distance.

6. Pratyahara

The restraining of the mind from the objects of senses is Pratyahara (subjugation of the senses).

Contemplating upon everything that one sees as Atman is Pratyahara. Renouncing the fruits of one's daily actions is Pratyahara. Turning away from all objects of sense is Pratyahara. Dharana in the eighteen important places of the body is Pratyahara. Drawing away of the organs from attaching themselves to the objects of senses is Pratyahara.

7. Dharana

The mind having drawn away from the objects of the senses, the fixing of the Chaitanya on one alone is Dharana.

There having made the mind one-pointed with thought, and the functions of the senses subdued, steady on his seat, he should practise Yoga for the purification of the Self.

As a lamp in a windless place flickereth not, to such is likened the Yogi of subdued thought, absorbed in the Yoga of Self.

As often as the wavering and unsteady mind goeth forth, so often receiving it in, let him bring it under the control of the Self.

8. Dhyana

The contemplation of the oneness of consciousness in all objects is Dhyana.

Not being troubled by any thoughts of the world then constitutes the Dhyana.

It is stated that Dhyana is the firm mind itself, devoid of Vasanas which are of the nature of Chintana (worrying thoughts).

Quiescence and Kaivalya pertain to this mind only.

9. Siddhis

Those, who not having full Jnana, are subject to bondage in this world, develop those powers (Siddhis) through medicines, Mantras, actions, time or skill; but these Siddhis do not pertain legitimately to a true Jnani.

Medicines, Mantras, etc., will but confer on one Siddhis, but never the beneficent Moksha.

For one who practises the best kind of Yoga and seeks union with Me, these Siddhis have been called obstacles and things that cause waste of time.

10. Samadhi

Separate the Manas from the body, and unite it with the Paramatman. This is known as Samadhi or Mukti from all states of consciousness.

Performing Manomurcha Kumbhaka, unite the Manas with the Atman. By this, Raja Yoga Samadhi is obtained.

Through the force of the practice of Dhyana, the current of the modification of Manas devoid of Self that is of Brahmic nature is said to be Samprajnata Samadhi, while the mind with the utter quiescence of modifications that confers upon one supreme bliss is said to be Asamprajnata Samadhi that is dear unto Yogins.

Forgetting oneself in Dhyana is Samadhi.

Know that when the mind, though performing all actions, is yet free from them, that state is termed the blissful Samadhi, the non-fluctuating Nirvana and the transcendent bliss.

Persons without full even-mindedness will never be able to go into Samadhi, even though they may comply with the formalities of sitting in Padma posture and offering salutations to Parabrahman. It is Atma Jnana alone which forming the Agni to the fuel of desires, constitutes the noble Samadhi. If the mind, being destroyed through concentration, cognises Tattva Jnana; such a Jnana is stated by the wise to be Samadhi.

With the disappearance of the attachment to the body and with the realisation of the Supreme Self, to whatever object the mind is directed one experiences Samadhi.

APPENDIX B

PSYCHIC INFLUENCE

1. Personality

In common parlance when one says that Dr. Tagore has a good personality, he means that Dr. Tagore has a strong, stalwart, tall figure, a beautiful complexion, a fine nose, sharp and lustrous eyes, broad chest, a muscular body, symmetrical limbs, curly hair and so on. That which distinguishes one man from another is personality. In reality, personality is something more than this. It includes a man's character, intelligence, noble qualities, moral conduct, intellectual attainments, certain striking faculties, special traits or characteristics, sweet powerful voice, etc. All these things put together constitute the personality of Mr. So and so. The sum total of all these things makes up the personality of a man. Mere physical characteristics cannot make up the personality.

What you call an umbrella is really a long stick plus a black cloth and some thin iron pieces. Similarly, what you call 'personality' is really the external physical body, plus brain and the nervous system and the mind which has its seat in the brain.

If one man is able to influence many people, we say that such and such a man has a magnetic personality. A full-blown Yogi or Jnani is the greatest personality in the world. He may be of a small stature. He may be ugly also. He may be clad in rags. And yet he is a mighty personality, a great Mahatma. People flock to him in thousands and pay homage to him. A man who has attained ethical perfection by the continued practice of right conduct or Yama and Niyama has also got a magnetic personality. He can

(194)

influence millions. But he is inferior to a Jnani or a Yogi who has got full knowledge of the Self.

Dr. Samuel Johnson had an awkward figure, a pot belly and unsymmetrical limbs. But he was the greatest personality of the age. He was neither a Yogi nor a Jnani. But he had intellectual attainments. He was a great essayist. He had good command of the English language. He was famous for his bombastic style. It was called Johnsonian English. Just hear some of his lines: "Will you be kind enough to allow my digits into your odoriferous concavity and extract therefrom some of the pulverised atoms which, ascending my nasal promontory, cause a great titillation of all my olfactory nerves?"

Rich people also have some personality. This is due to the 'Money-power'. They may be licentious. Money has its own share in the making up of the personality of man. It infuses in him a sort of colouring. The charitable nature may cover up their licentious nature and may send some fragrance abroad. People flock to them. Lord Jesus says: "Charity covereth a multitude of sins."

Character gives a strong personality to man. People respect a man who has a good character. Moral people command respect everywhere. He who is honest, sincere, truthful, kind and liberal-hearted always commands respect and influence at the hands of people. Sattvic virtues make a man divine. He who speaks truth and practises Brahmacharya becomes a great and dynamic personality. Even if he speaks a word, there is power in it and people are magnetised. Character-building is of paramount importance if a man wants to develop his personality. Brahmacharya is the root of a magnetic personality. No development of a strong personality is possible without celibacy.

Personality can be developed. Practice of virtues is indispensable. One should try to be always cheerful. A morose, gloomy man cannot attract and influence people.

He is an infectious parasite amidst society. He spreads gloom everywhere. A man of a jolly nature with the spirit of service, with humility and obedience can influence millions. The law of "like attracts like" operates in the physical and mental planes. A man of strong personality need not send invitations to people. Just as bees come and perch as soon as flowers blossom, so also people of lesser mind are attracted to men of strong personality, of their own accord.

A powerful, sweet voice, knowledge of music, knowledge of astrology, astronomy, palmistry, art, etc., add to the personality of a man. One should know how to behave and adjust himself with other people. You must talk sweetly and gently. This produces a tremendous impression. You must be polite, civil, courteous. You must treat others with respect and consideration. He who gives respect to others gets respect. Humility brings respect by itself. Humility is a virtue that subdues the hearts of others. A man of humility is a powerful magnet or loadstone.

You must know the ways to approach people. You must know how to talk with them and how to behave towards them. Behaviour is most important. An arrogant, stubborn and self-willed man can never become a man of strong personality. He is disliked by all.

Develop joyful nature. Always keep a smiling and cheerful face. This will give you a good personality. People will like you much. Your superiors will be very much pleased. Have an amiable nature, a modest and unassuming temperament. You will succeed in your interviews with all big guns. Take down notes of what you want to speak with them in the course of the interview. Keep a small memorandum slip in your pocket. Remember the points well and talk slowly and gently. Then the man will patiently hear. Do not be agitated in your talks. Do not become nervous. Be bold. Pay respects with sincerity as soon as you see the person. Do not stand erect like the proverbial man who holds the gas-light in a marriage procession. Gently bow your head with feeling. The man will be immensely pleased. He will be glad to receive you with a depth of feeling and you will get success in your interview. Talk about the important points first and just review in your mind whether you have finished all the points you wanted to talk. In the West, people care for personality. In India, people care for individuality and assert: *"Aham Asmi"* —which means "I exist." They try to destroy the personality to realise the Self.

Endeavour to possess a magnetic personality. Try to possess that strange and mysterious power, personal magnetism which charms and fascinates people. Understand the secrets of personal influence. Develop your will-power. Conserve all leaking energy. Enjoy robust, blooming health and a high standard of vigour and vitality and achieve social and financial success in every walk of life. If you can understand the amazing secrets of personal influence, you can increase the earning capacity and can have a broader and happier life.

A strong personality is a very valuable asset for you. You can develop it if you will. "Where there is a will there is a way" is a maxim which is as true today as it was from the time of Adam. Win laurels of name and fame and attain success in life through a dynamic personality. You can do it. You must do it. You know the science now. I shall back you up.

2. Power of Suggestions

You should have a clear understanding of suggestions and their effects upon the mind. You should be careful in the use of suggestion. Never give wrong suggestion which will have destructive results to anybody. You will be doing a great harm and a disservice to him. Think well before you speak. Teachers and professors should have a thorough knowledge of the Science of Suggestion and Autosuggestion. Then they can educate and elevate students in an efficient manner. In Southern India, when children cry out in houses, parents frighten them by saying: "Look here, Balu! Irendukannan has come (The two-eyed man has come). Keep quiet. Or I will hand you over to this man." "Puchandi (or ghost) has come" and suggestions of this sort are very destructive. The child becomes timid. The minds of children are elastic, tender and pliable. Samskaras are indelibly impressed at this age. Changing or obliterating the Samskaras becomes impossible when they grow. When the child grows into a man, he manifests timidity. Parents should infuse courage into the minds of their children. They should say: "Here is a lion. See the lion in this picture. Roar like a lion. Be courageous. See the picture of Shivaji, Arjuna or Clive. Become chivalrous." In the West, teachers show the pictures of battlefields to children and say: "Look here, James! See this picture of Napoleon. Look at his cavalry. Won't you like to become a Commander-in-Chief of the army or a Brigadier-General?" They infuse courage into the minds of children from their very childhood. When they grow, these Samskaras get strengthened by additional external stimuli.

Doctors should have a thorough knowledge of the science of suggestion. Sincere, sympathetic doctors are very rare. Doctors who have no knowledge of suggestion do more harm than good. They kill patients sometimes by unnecessarily frightening them. If there is a little cough of an ordinary nature, the doctor says: "Now, my friend, you have got T.B. You must go to Bhowali or Switzerland or Vienna. You must go in for a course of tuberculin injections." Poor patient is frightened. There is not at all any sign of consumption. The case is an ordinary one. It is simple catarrh of the chest from exposure to chills. The patient actually develops phthisis by fright and worry owing to the wrong destructive suggestion of the doctor. The doctor ought to have told him: "Oh, it is nothing. It is simple cold. You will be all right by tomorrow. Take a purgative and inhale a little oil of eucalyptus. Adjust your diet. It is better you fast today." Such a doctor is God Himself. He must be adored. A doctor may say now: "Well, sir, if I say so, I will lose my practice. I cannot pull on in this world." This is a mistake. Truth always gains victory. People will run to you as you are sympathetic and kind. You will have a roaring practice.

There is healing by suggestion. This is a drugless treatment. This is suggestive therapeutics. By good and powerful suggestion, you can cure any disease. You will have to learn this science and practise it. All doctors of Homoeopathic, Allopathic, Ayurvedic and Unani systems should know this science. They can combine this system along with their own systems. They will have a roaring practice by this happy combination.

Do not be easily influenced by the suggestions of others. Have your own sense of individuality. A strong suggestion, though it does not influence the subject immediately, will operate in due course. It will never go in vain.

We all live in a world of suggestions. Our character is daily modified unconsciously by association with others. We unconsciously imitate the actions of those whom we admire. We daily absorb the suggestions of those with whom we come in daily contact. We are acted upon by these suggestions. A man of weak mind yields to the suggestions of a man of strong mind.

The servant is always under the influence of the suggestions of his master. The wife is under the influence of the suggestions of her husband. The patient is under the influence of the suggestions of the doctor. The student is under the influence of the teacher. Custom is nothing but the product of suggestion. The dress that you put on, the manners, the behaviour and even the food that you eat are all the outcome of suggestions only. Nature suggests in various ways. The running rivers, the shining sun, fragrant flowers, the growing trees, are all incessantly sending you suggestions.

All the prophets of yore were hypnotists. They knew the science of suggestion fully well. Their words had tremendous powers. Every word they uttered had magic power and a peculiar charm. All the hearers remained spell-bound. A spiritual preacher produces a sort of hypnosis in the minds of others. The hearers come under the influence of his suggestions.

There is power in every word that is spoken. There are two kinds of Vrittis, *viz.,* Sakti-Vritti and Lakshana-Vritti in words. In the Upanishads, the Lakshana-Vritti is taken. "Vedasvarupoham" does not mean "embodiment of Vedas." The Lakshana-Vritti does denote "Brahman" who can be reached by the study of the Upanishads alone: by the Sabda Pramana alone.

Mark here the power in the words. If anyone calls another "Sala" or "Badmash" or "fool," he is thrown into a state of fury immediately. Fight ensues. If you address anyone as "Bhagavan" or "Prabhu" or "Maharaj," he is immensely pleased.

3. Hypnotism and Mesmerism

A greater mind can influence a smaller mind. This is mesmerism or hypnotism. This is not at all a new science. It is also Anaadi. It has existed from beginningless time. It was only Mesmer and Braid who popularised this science in the West. Hindu Rishis knew this science in days long gone by. Demosthenes and Socrates, Visvamitra and Patanjali Maharshi used hypnotism and mesmerism in olden days. It was James Braid, the Manchester surgeon, who gave this name hypnotism to this science and who first founded this science in the West. The term 'hypnotism' has a Greek origin which means sleep.

Mesmer was a philosopher, physician and astrologer.

He was born in 1784. He died in 1815. He brought in the
theory of animal magnetism. He believed that man had a
wonderful magnetic power by which he could heal and
influence other people. He made use of this power in the
treatment of various diseases. The system of mesmerism is
known after his name.

All orators possess the power of hypnotism.
Consciously or unconsciously they subdue the minds of
hearers. The hearers are swayed by the powerful speech of
orators. They are charmed, as it were, for the time being.
All the religious preachers and prophets of the world
possessed this power to a remarkable degree.

Suggestion is the master-key to hypnotism. The
hypnotist suggests and the operator acts implicitly. The
lesser mind implicitly obeys the higher mind. Suggestion is
an idea communicated by the operator to the subject.
Suggestion is a science. One should be very clever in
putting the suggestion in a skilful manner. We live in the
world of suggestion and under the magic spell and
influence of hypnotism. Hypnotism is a mighty power in
the world. We are all hypnotised by the spell of Maya. We
will have to dehypnotise ourselves to obtain a knowledge
of the Self. Vedanta gives powerful suggestions to
dehypnotise ourselves. Hypnotism is a state of mind in
which suggestions, verbal and visual, are received as true
whether they are true or not. There is an irresistible desire
to carry out the suggestions. The power of will and the
power of suggestion are very closely linked together.

The operator develops his power of hypnosis through
the practice of crystal-gazing and other methods of
concentration. Pranayama also helps a lot in the
development of this power. Brahmacharya also is very
essential. A man of loose character cannot become a
powerful hypnotist.

A man can be hypnotised by gazing or suggestion or
passes. The operator makes some 'passes' in front of the

subject and the subject passes into a hypnotic state. The passes in the reverse direction will bring back the subject to normal consciousness. Sometimes, if the hypnotist is a powerful man, he can hypnotise several persons in a group or bunch. That man who resists the suggestions of the hypnotist cannot be hypnotised so easily. If one believes in the hypnotiser and thinks he can be hypnotised, he can rapidly come under his spell and operation.

There is also another variety of hypnotism called the stage hypnotism in which the hypnotist hypnotises the whole audience and shows several tricks. He puts a lady in a small tight box in standing posture, ties her hands and closes the box and then cuts the box with a saw. Afterwards he opens the broken box and the lady comes out without any injury. A famous Fakir ascended the platform in England with a red rope in his hand, threw it in the air and climbed up through the rope and then vanished in the air. This is stage-hypnotism. This is the famous 'rope-trick' of the Fakir. There was no impression in the plate of a camera. This is a trick only after all. A hypnotist hypnotises a boy and places his head and feet over two chairs. He then places a large weight over his body. The body does not bend. He asks the audience to clasp the fingers of both hands and makes a strong current of electricity to pass. They all actually feel the shock of the current. He first starts the current in his own hands and thinks strongly that the current should pass to the hands of others.

Hypnotism is very beneficial in the correction of bad habits of boys and in the treatment of hysteria and other nervous diseases. The opium habit and the drinking habit are also removed. The hypnotist should not misuse the power in wrong channels. He will get a hopeless downfall. Wherever there is power, there is side by side a chance for misuse. There are temptations also. One has to be very careful.

A hypnotist looks at the second-hand of a watch and

the second-hand stops immediately. He asks a subject to look at the second-hand of a watch and stops his thinking. His eyes becomes listless. A hypnotist makes the body of a hypnotised subject to levitate and move in the air through a big iron ring. The hypnotised person is blindfolded. He is able to walk over a rope that is distributed on the ground in quite a zigzag manner. He is able to read the contents of a sealed letter and give proper answers to questions. Here the unconscious mind of the subject operates. He can see through an opaque wall. Marvellous are the mysteries of the science of hypnotism! Thanks to Mr. James Braid of happy memory!

4. Telepathy

Telepathy is thought-transference from one person to another. Just as sound moves in the ethereal space, so also thought moves in the mental space, Chidakasa. There is an ocean of ether all round. There is also an ocean of mind all round. Thought has shape, colour, weight and form. It is as much matter as this pencil. When you have some good thought of an elevating nature sometimes, it is very difficult to say whether it is your own thought or the thought of some other person. Thoughts of other persons enter your brain.

Telepathy was the first wireless telegraphy of the Yogis. Yogis send their messages through telepathy. Thought travels with electric speed that is unimaginable. Sometimes you think of a friend with such intensity in the evening that you get a letter from him early in the morning. This is unconscious telepathy. Your powerful thought has travelled and reached the brain of your friend immediately and he has replied you then and there. So many interesting and wonderful things are going on in the thought-world. Ordinarily, people who have not developed the power of telepathy are groping in the darkness.

Telepathy is communication of mind with mind. The

pineal gland which is considered by occultists as the seat of the soul plays an important part in telepathy. It is this pineal gland that actually receives messages. It is a small piece of nervous matter that is imbedded in the brain or hind-brain in the floor of the mind ventricle. It is an endocrine gland that is ductless. It has got an internal secretion which is directly poured into the blood.

Practise telepathy in the beginning from a short distance. It is better to practise at nights, to start with. Ask your friend to have the receptive attitude and concentration at ten o'clock. Ask him to sit on Virasana or Padmasana with closed eyes in a dark room. Try to send your message exactly at the appointed time. Concentrate on the thoughts that you want to send. Will strongly now. The thoughts will leave your brain and enter the brain of your friend. There may be some mistakes in the beginning here and there. When you advance in practice and know the technique well, you will always be correct in sending and receiving messages. Later on, you will be able to forward messages to different corners of the world. Thought-waves vary in intensity and force. The sender and receiver should practise great and intense concentration. Then there will be force in sending the messages, clarity and accuracy in receiving the messages. Practise in the beginning telepathy from one room to the next room in the same house. This science is very pleasant and interesting. It needs patient practice. Brahmacharya is very essential.

You can influence another man without any audible language. What is wanted is concentration of thought that is directed by the will. This is telepathy. Here is an exercise for your practice in telepathy. Think of your friend or cousin who is living in a distant land. Bring a clear-cut image of his face to your mind. If you have his photo look at it and speak to it audibly. When you retire to bed think of the picture with intense concentration. He will write to you the desired letter the following day or so. Try this yourself. Do not doubt. You will be quite surprised. You will get success and firm conviction in the science of telepathy. Sometimes, when you are writing something or reading a newspaper, suddenly you get a message from some one near and dear to you. You think of him suddenly. He has sent you a message. He has thought of you seriously. Thought-vibrations travel faster than light or electricity. In such instances, the subconscious mind receives the messages or impressions and transmits the same to the conscious mind.

Great adepts or Mahatmas who live in the Himalayan caves transmit their messages through telepathy to deserving aspirants or Yogis in the world. These Jijnasus or Yogis carry out their orders and disseminate their knowledge far and wide. It is not necessary that Mahatmas should come on the platform and preach. Whether they preach or not, it does not matter. Their very life is an embodiment of teaching. They are the living assurance for God-realisation. Preaching on the platform belongs to the second-class type of men who have no knowledge of telepathy. The hidden Yogis help the world through their spiritual vibrations and magnetic aura more than the Yogis of the platform. In these days, worldly people expect even Sannyasins to work on the political platform. They even force them. As their minds are saturated with Karma Samskaras, they are not able to grasp and understand the grandeur, utility and magnanimity of pure Nivritti of Dhyana-Yogis. The field or domain of activity of Sannyasins is entirely different. They cannot become presidents of Sabhas or Mandalas. Their sphere is of a cosmic nature. Their field is Adhyatmic that relates to the science of the Self. Let me repeat the words of Bhagavan Sri Krishna:

"Lokesmin dvividha nishtha pura prokta mayanagha,
Jnanayogena samkhyanam karmayogena yoginam."

"In this world there is a twofold path, as I said before,

O sinless one, that of Yoga by Knowledge, of the Sankhyas, and that of Yoga by action, of the Yogis" (Gita, III-3). The glory of Hinduism will be lost, if Sannyasins become extinct. They can never become extinct from India. The Samskaras of Tyaga and renunciation are ingrained in their cells, nerves and tissues. Buddhists have got monks. Mohammedans have their Fakirs. Christians have got their priests, clergymen and reverend fathers. Every religion has people in the world with the spirit of renunciation. There must be a set of people in every religion who are entirely devoted to divine contemplation. It is the duty of householders to attend to their wants. They will receive their blessings. It is these people who lead the life of Nivritti Marga, who can make researches in Yoga and give to the world new messages. It is these men who can really help the world at large and do Loka-Kalyana.

5. Clairvoyance

Clairvoyance is vision of distant objects through the inner astral eye or psychic eye. Just as you have physical sense in the physical body, there are astral counterparts of these Indriyas in the inner, subtle, astral body. The Yogi or the occultist develops these inner organs through practice of concentration. He develops clairvoyant vision. He can see objects in far-off climes. This Siddhi or power is called Dura Drishti.

Just as light rays penetrate a glass, just as X-rays penetrate solid, opaque objects, so also the Yogi can see the things through a solid wall, can see the contents of a sealed envelope and the contents of a hidden treasure underneath the ground through his inner psychic eye. This psychic eye is the eye of intuition or Divya Drishti or Jnana-Chakshus. One has to develop this inner eye through concentration. Just as the microscope magnifies the small cells, germs, etc., so also he can see things of the astral world very clearly through this inner eye and can magnify them also by special focussing of the inner astral lens.

He creates an astral tube by willing and the strong wishing and thinking and, through this astral tube, he sees things at a distance. The vision may not be very clear in the beginning. Just as the new-born baby learns, so also he learns in the beginning. As he advances in his practice, his inner vision becomes quite distinct. There is another method. The Yogi takes astral journey and sees things during his astral travelling unconsciously.

Just as light rays travel in space, so also astral light rays travel with tremendous velocity. They are caught up by the astral eye. Every one of you has got these astral senses. But few only consciously develop them. A clairvoyant can see the events of the past by looking into the Akasic records and have Trikala Jnana also. The degree of power varies in different individuals. Advanced clairvoyants are very rare.

6. Clairaudience

Clairaudience is the hearing of distant sounds in the astral plane by means of the astral ear. The process is similar to clairvoyance. The astral sound-vibrations are caught hold of by the astral sense of hearing. A clairvoyant need not necessarily be a clairaudiant. These are two distinct powers.

Patanjali Maharshi gives the method to develop this power of distant hearing. *"Srotrakasayoh sambandha-samyamaddivyam srotram"* (Patanjali Yoga Sutras, III-42). By Samyama on the relation between the ear and Akasa (ether), comes divine hearing. Samyama is concentration and meditation combined.

All the inhabitants of the Pitriloka possess this power. Where their descendants perform Sraaddha and Tarpana in this world, they hear these sounds through the power of clairaudience and they are highly pleased.

These psychic Siddhis are all by-products of

concentration. Just as there are various coal-tar derivatives and various petroleum preparations, so also there are these Siddhis manifest in a Yogi when he concentrates. These are all obstacles in the path of spirituality. The aspirant should ignore them and develop Vairagya. Then only will he be able to reach the goal.

All the sound vibrations of the past are in the Akasic records. The Yogi can hear these sounds nicely. He can hear the sounds of Shakespeare, Johnson, Valmiki, Visvamitra, etc. Just as you can hear now the music and song of a songster who died fifty years ago in the gramophonic records, so also the Yogi can hear the sounds of those persons of the past by concentration connecting his astral hearing to the Akasic records. Just as impressions of your boyhood remain in your brain and the subconscious mind, so also the impressions of old sounds remain in the Akasic records. One should know the Yogis' technique only. Just as the experienced record-keeper in the office can bring out in a short time any old record, so also the Yogi can hear the sound of good old days in the twinkling of an eye.

GLOSSARY

ABHAVA: Absence; disappearance.
Abhimana: Egoistic identification.
Abhinivesha: Clinging to life.
Abhivyakta: Manifestation.
Abhyantara: Internal.
Abhyasa: Spiritual practice.
Adhimatra: Intense.
Ahamkara: Egoism; self-assertive principle.
Ahimsa: Non-killing; abstinence from injury.
Akasa: Ether.
Alambana: Support.
Alpa: Little.
Anaadi: Beginningless.
Anagata: Future.
Ananda: Bliss; happiness.
Ananta: Infinite.
Aneka: Many.
Anga: Accessories; limbs.
Anima: The Siddhi by which the Yogi can become minute.
Anitya: Non-eternal.
Anta: End.
Antahkarana: The fourfold internal instrument viz.,
    mind, Buddhi, Chitta and Ahamkara.
Antaranga: Internal.
Antarmukha: Inward.
Anusandhana: Enquiry.
Anushthana: Sustained practice.
Anvaya: Qualities.
Anyatha: Separate.
Artha: Meaning; purpose; objects.
Asana: Posture; seat.
Asmita: Egoism.
Asteya: Abstinence from theft.

Asuddhi: Impurity.
Atyanta: Complete.
Aushadhi: Herbs; medicine; drug.
Avarana: Covering; veil of ignorance.
Avidya: Ignorance.
Avyakritam: Undifferentiated.

BAHIRANGA: External.
Bahya: External.
Bala: Strength.
Bhavana: Feeling.
Bheda: Difference.
Bhoga: Life-experience; enjoyment.
Bhranti Darshana: Mistaken notion.
Bhuta: Elements.
Bhuvana: World.
Bija: Seed.
Brahmachari: Celibate.
Brahmacharya: Continence; celibacy.
Buddhi: Intellect.

CHAITANYA: Consciousness; intelligence.
Chakra: Lotus; plexus; wheel.
Chakshu: Eye.
Chandra: Moon.
Chintana: Thinking.
Chitsakti: Power of consciousness.
Chitta: Mind-stuff; organ of memory.

DARSHAN: The instrument of seeing; vision.
Daurmanasya: Despair.
Desa: Place.
Devata: Deity.
Dhairya: Endurance; patience.
Dharana: Concentration.
Dharma: Characterestics.
Dharmi: Substratum; that which possesses the Dharma.
Dhruva: Pole-star.
Dhyana: Meditation.
Divya: Luminous; supernatural.
Doshas: Faults.
Drik: The seer.

Drishta: The visible; seen.
Duhkha: Pain; misery.
Dvandva: Pairs of opposites.
Dvesha: Hatred.

EKA: One.
Ekagrata: One-pointed; concentrated.

GARIMA: The Siddhi by which the Yogi becomes very heavy.
Gauna: Secondary.
Grahana: Power of cognition.
Grahya: Capable of receiving.
Guna: Qualities.

HANA: Destruction.
Hasti: Elephant.
Hetu: Cause.
Hridaya: Heart.

INDRIYAS: Organs.
Isatvam: The Siddhi by which the Yogi becomes the Lord.

JAGRAT: Waking state.
Jala: Not real; jugglery.
Janma: Births.
Japa: Repetition of a Mantra.
Jati: Species; class.
Jiva: Human being; individual soul.
Jnana Indriyas: Organs of knowledge, viz., ear, skin, eye,
   tongue and nose.
Jnana: Knowledge.

KAIVALYA: Absolute independence.
Kala: Time.
Kantha: Throat.
Karana: Instrument.
Karma Indriyas: Organs of actions, viz., mouth, hand, feet,
   genitals and anus.
Karma: Action.
Karuna: Mercy.
Kaya-vyuha: Group of bodies.
Kaya: Physical body.
Kevala: Alone.
Klesha: Affliction.

Krama: Succession.
Kriya Yoga: Yoga of action; purification.
Krodha: Anger.
Kshama: Mercy; forgiveness.
Kshana: Moment.
Kshaya: Destruction; annihilation.
Kshetra: Field; source.
Kshina: Powerless.
Kumbhaka: Retention of breath.

LAGHIMA: The Siddhi by which the Yogi can become lighter.
Lakshana: Sign.
Laya: Dissolution.
Linga Sarira: Astral body.
Linga: Mark.
Lobha: Greed.
Loka Sangraha: Uplift of humanity.

MADHYAMA: Middle.
Maha: Great.
Mahatva: Infinity.
Mahima: The Siddhi by which the Yogi can become infinite.
Maitri: Friendliness.
Manas: Mind.
Manasic Japa: Mental repetition of a Mantra.
Manonasa: Annihilation of mind.
Mantra: Incantations.
Matra: A unit; alone.
Maya: Illusive power of Isvara.
Moha: Delusion.
Mula: Origin.

NABHI CHAKRA: Manipura Chakra.
Nabhi: Navel.
Nidra: Deep sleep.
Nimitta: Incidental cause.
Niralamba: Supportless.
Nirbija: Seedless (without Samskaras).
Nirmana: Created.
Nirodha: Restraint; suppression.
Nirvichara: Without argumentation.
Nitya: Eternal.

Nivritti: Removal.
Niyama: Observance, the second step of Raja Yoga.
OJAS: Spiritual energy.
PARA: Other energy.
Parakaya Pravesa: Entering into another body.
Parama: Higher; supreme.
Parinama: Transformation; modification; change.
Paroksha: Direct.
Phala: Fruits.
Pradhana: Chief.
Prajna: Consciousnes; discrimination.
Prakasa: Luminous; light.
Prakriti-layas: Those who are submerged.
Prakriti: Nature.
Pramana: Right knowledge.
Prana: Vital energy.
Pranajaya: Conquest of Prana.
Pranava: The sacred syllable OM.
Pranayama: Control of Prana.
Pranidhana: Self-surrender.
Prapti: The Siddhi by which the Yogi can obtain
    all the desired things.
Prasvasa: Expiratory breath.
Pratibandha: Obstacles.
Pratibha: Intuition.
Pratipaksha: Opposite.
Pratiptasava: Becoming latent.
Pratyahara: Abstraction of the senses.
Pratyaya: Cause; mental effort; imitation; idea of distinction.
Pravritti: Activity.
Prayatna: Effort.
RAGA: Attachment, like.
Rajas: Passion.
Ratna: Wealth.
Rechaka: Exhalation.
Rupa: Form; beauty.
SABDHA: Word.
Sadhaka: Spiritual aspirant.
Sadhana: Spiritual practices.

Sakti: Power; energy.
Sama: Equality.
Samadhi: Superconscious state; trance.
Samapatti: End.
Samaya: Circumstance.
Sambandha: Relation; connection.
Sampat: Perfection.
Samsaya: Doubt.
Samskaras: Mental impressions.
Samvit: Knowledge.
Sanga: Attachment; association.
Sankalpa: Thought.
Santa: Peaceful; calm.
Santosha: Contentment.
Sarupyam: Luminous; identification.
Sarvajna: All-knowing; omniscient.
Sarvam: All.
Satsanga: Association with the wise.
Sattva: Purity.
Satya: Truthfulness.
Saucha: Purity.
Savichara: With deliberation.
Savitarka: Without argumentation.
Siddha: Perfected soul.
Siddhi: Psychic powers.
Smriti: Memory.
Sravana: Hearing the srutis; clairaudience.
Srotra: Ear.
Sthiti: Steadiness.
Sthula: Gross.
Suddha: Pure.
Sukha: Happiness.
Sukshma: Subtle.
Sunya: Destitute of; devoid of.
Svabhasana: Self-luminous.
Svadhyaya: Study of scriptures.
Svapna: Dream.
Svarupa: One's own nature.
Svasa: Inspiratory breath.

TAMAS: Inertia.
Tapas: Austerity; mortification.
Taraka Jnana: The knowledge that leads to Moksha.
Tejas: Agni; fire.
Tivra: Keen; intense.
Trishna: Thirsting for objects.

UPARAGA: Colouring.
Upasaka: One who meditates.
Upasarga: Obstacles.
Upaya: Means.

VAIKHARI: Verbal chanting of a Mantra.
Vairagya: Dispassion; non-attachment.
Vaitrishnyam: Non-attachment.
Vajra: Adamantine firmness.
Vasana: Desire.
Vasikara: Control.
Vasitvam: Deliberation.
Vastu: Objects.
Vibhu: All-pervading.
Vichara: Enquiry into the nature of Atman.
Videha: Bodiless.
Vikalpa: Fancy; Imagination.
Viniyoga: Application.
Vipareetha Bhavana: Perverted understanding.
Viparyaya: Wrong knowledge; wrong cognition.
Virodha: Opposing.
Visesha: Distinction; defined.
Vishaya: Objects.
Visoka: Without sorrow.
Vitaraga: One who is desireless.
Viveka: Discrimination.
Vritti: Modification of mind; thought-wave.

YAMA: Restraint.
Yoga Darshana: Yoga philosophy.
Yogarudha: One who is established in Yoga.
Yogyata: Fitness.

APPENDIX D

REFERENCE TO SUTRAS

CHAPTER I

SAMADHIPADA

CHAPTER II

SADHANAPADA

CHAPTER III

VIBHUTIPADA